T0351429

Comedies

THE GERMAN LIST

Comedies

ROBERT WALSER

TRANSLATED BY

DANIELE PANTANO AND JAMES REIDEL

LONDON NEW YORK CALCUTTA

This publication was supported by a grant from the Goethe-Institut India

Seagull Books, 2018

Originally published as *Komödie. Märchenspiele und szenische Dichtungen* by Robert Walser © Suhrkamp Verlag, Berlin 2016

Grateful acknowledgement is made for 'The Lovers', 'Poets' and 'The Pond', which first appeared in *Conjunctions* 60 (2013); and to New Directions for 'The Christ Child', 'Cinderella', 'Snow White' and 'Thorn Rose, or Sleeping Beauty', which first appeared in the volume *Fairy Tales* (2015).

First published in English translation by Seagull Books, 2018

ISBN 978 0 8574 2 469 3

British Library Cataloguing-in-Publication Data
A catalogue record for this book is available from the British Library.

Typeset and designed by Seagull Books, Calcutta, India
Printed and bound by Maple Press, York, Pennsylvania, USA

CONTENTS

Translators' Note *vii*

PART I – The Pond **1**
The Pond (1898) 3

PART II – Early Dramolettes **17**
The Boys (1900) 19
Poets (1901) 31

PART III – Fairy Tales **41**
Cinderella (1901) 43
Snow White (1901) 92
Thorn Rose, or the Sleeping Beauty (1920) 137

PART IV – Later Dramolettes **149**
The Christ Child (1920) 151
The Lovers (1921) 165
The Good-for-Nothing (1922) 190

PART V – Felix **199**
The 'Felix' Scenes (1925) 201

Afterword *251*
No Standing Room:
Robert Walser's Theatre of Poetry and Fairy Tale
RETO SORG

TRANSLATORS' NOTE

The plays in this volume are taken from Robert Walser (1878–1956), *Komödie: Märchenspiele und szenische Dichtungen* (1986), an expanded collection of plays published in 1919. Aside from the English renderings and footnotes where necessary, a marked change from the source text is the order that was the subject of much scholarly debate since Walser's death in 1956. In this collection, the English texts follow a thematic arrangement after the 'autobiographical document' we found in researching and translating these plays. Thus, the first part of this collection begins with 'The Pond' [Der Teich], a play that, if not the earliest work, represents the earliest point at which Walser draws from his youth. The second part continues Walser's self-portrait in 'The Boys' [Die Knaben] and 'Poets' [Dichter]. The third part comprises the 'fairy-tale' plays from Walser's ambitious Berlin period: 'Cinderella' [Aschenbrödel], 'Snow White' [Schneewittchen] and a later dramolette, 'Thorn Rose, or the Sleeping Beauty' [Dornröschen]. The fourth part, consisting of later dramolettes, begins with 'The Christ Child' [Das Christkind] (which we included as a fairy tale in an earlier volume by New Directions). It is followed by plays with an autobiographical—and adult—cadence: 'The Lovers' [Das Liebespaar] is based on Walser's failed romance with Frieda Mermet; and 'The Good-for-Nothing' [Der Taugenichts] is representative of the way Walser played—toyed—with his sense of failure as a kind of success from the standpoint of self-awareness, self-analysis and self- pathologizing. The fifth part comprises the 'Felix' scenes, originally written in Walser's miniature script (*Mikrogramme*), a work that stands apart but creates a full circle, in which Walser returns to writing about his youth and family life.

The art of translation is like painting over a painting with hope that the rendering doesn't peel from the surface underneath. Exactitude, of course, is impossible. Perhaps it might be better to see what we have done as a kind of theatre, too, where the translators understudy the author's text and 'perform' it in English. If we did not stray from our roles, the reader should see what Robert Musil saw as this 'atmosphere of marionettes, romantic irony', that 'very human kind of playfulness, gentle, dreamy and free'. We also wanted that intensity, of a programme, which Walter Benjamin saw in Walser, that is, what Walser could have achieved as a writer and exemplar of the modern condition. Ultimately, we wanted to retain Walser's subtlety of language, which poses a real challenge to the translator's art. This is especially true of how Walser composes his realm of the idealized and damaged past in which he felt more at home—his 'safe space' as it were, with its utter lack of safety—which is always a presence to him, where he is always poring over Schiller and Goethe, seeing them performed on stage and in his head, where he hardly suffers the anxiety of their influence save his own.

PART I

The Pond

THE POND

(1898)*

A room. FRITZ *appears.*

FRITZ. I'd soon rather be nowhere than just be here. Nothing but wicked faces. That's how it is at the dinner table. Nothing but a clatter of spoons and forks and knives. Not a word. Only this timid whispering, this furtive clinking of glasses, this suffocated laughter. You can't open your mouth for fear of making a bad impression. What's the point of such impressions? Paul, he can talk, he gets away with everything. Everything about him is nice, good, proper, kind. He's the nicest boy in the world. Makes me feel like he's Mother's only son, like she has no other. I can't do anything right, no matter what I do. Fine, if that is how they want it. It's true, I'm so damned stubborn and sulky. If only they knew how I feel inside. If just once Mother could

*The late Jochen Greven, the editor of Walser's collected works, at one time asserted the earliest date of composition to be before Walser left home in 1895. That a fourteen-year-old could write such a play—that has been called a 'symbolic analysis' of his own creativity—was subsequently challenged by Bernhard Echte who examined Walser's handwriting and literary development, which places the composition no later than 1902. This led Greven to compromise at 1898 or 1900. Our placement sides with neither. We see it as an outlier to Walser's *oeuvre* and never intended for see into my heart. She'd probably be surprised, she'd probably see that I too love her a little. Oh—love her! What else could I say? There's no need for a single word. I know it, but it's sad that no one else does. I need to go up to my room and think about it all. I'll probably start crying. So what? Nobody will see it. Crying's only crying when someone's there and hears it. Let's go, Fritzi, let's get out of the way.

He wants to leave. KLARA, *his sister, appears.*

KLARA. What are you doing standing around here?

FRITZ. Well, you have to stand somewhere. Anyway, what do you care?

KLARA. I'm going to tell Papa.

FRITZ. Go ahead! I'm not afraid of him!

KLARA. Oh? And what if I tell Mama? You're still not afraid?

FRITZ. Don't be such a tattletale. That's mean.

KLARA. I'm going to tell her.

FRITZ. Whatever. Let her clock me on the head. Let the whole world clock me on the head, for all I care.

KLARA. I'm going to tell! You just wait.

FRITZ. You're a stupid— (*Horrified, he pauses.*)

publication. In fact, 'The Pond' (*Der Teich*) was for the private amusement of his sister Fanny. Furthermore, its strangeness—this *narzißtischen Autismus* as one scholar termed it—and that it was written in *Berndeutsch,* make it a further curiosity, as Walser claimed to have never composed any of his work in his native dialect, seeing it as 'unseemly'. That said, it is impossible to convey the dialect in a translation. However, if one considers that English shares so many loanwords and cognates with other languages, especially German and French, then, perhaps, one could say that a *dialect* is ever present in English.

KLARA. I'm a what? You were going to call me a stupid cow, right? A stupid cow! I'm going to tell, I'm going to tell.

MRS MARTI *appears.*

KLARA. Mama, Fritz called me a stupid cow again.

MRS MARTI. Shut up! (*To* FRITZ) Come here! (*To* KLARA) Get to work. March.

MRS MARTI *and* FRITZ *go into the other room.*

KLARA (*sits down at the worktable*). What a pig! He's going to get it twenty times over again. He always overdoes it. What does he think, we won't ever say anything? That we can't open our mouths? (*Screaming can be heard.*) Ah, how he's crying now! Like an ox about to be slaughtered. What a big lad! He should be ashamed.

MRS MARTI *enters.*

MRS MARTI. Next time you'll get it too, you tattletale. Shame on you for always moaning. That's not nice. I have better things to do than always listen to you moan. You should just keep quiet sometimes.

KLARA. But when he always—

MRS MARTI. Be quiet. You should be ashamed of yourself. And stop bothering me with this. I don't want to hear about it any more. Understood? (*Leaves.*)

FRITZ *appears cautiously.*

KLARA. Come in, she's gone. You got it good, didn't you? So are you going to call me a stupid cow again?

FRITZ *leaves silently.*

KLARA. He's had enough!—But I should hurry to get this work done, so I can go and play outside. I love being outside, where there's not always a fuss like in here. What time is it? Already three? Go, hurry, hurry.

A street.

FRITZ. *At some distance*, FRANZ, HEINRICH, OTTO *and other boys*.

FRITZ. I'm tired of standing around. But I can't stand it at home. What's there for me? I can't just sit in my room all day.

OTTO. Hey, Fritz, are you coming with us?

FRITZ (*to himself*). I would like to run and play. But I can't stop thinking about it. Thinking about the same thing. I'd rather be alone.

HEINRICH. We're asking you to come with us! Can't you hear? Lost your voice?

FRITZ. They just get on my nerves and bore me to death. Why am I such a droop head?

FRANZ. Just leave this clown alone, who's better than everybody. Come on, let's go without the scholar.

HEINRICH. Sit down, Fritz, and look up into the sky, you dreamer. (*They leave.*)

FRITZ. If they're so good without me, then why do they bother asking me along? They should just go. I don't even want to know about it, really. I like being alone. That's when you can think. Nobody bothers you. I always feel like I've lost something somewhere. I know it's nothing, but it still worries me. What could it be? Nothing? What am I saying! It's something, but stupid me forgot what it was. I want to follow this train. I want to find my place in the forest. Maybe there I'll remember it. It will come to me like a butterfly. Anyway, why do I have to think? I have to, I'm forced to. Isn't it stupid that you have to do something?

You shouldn't have to do anything. But I'm the one to talk. Come on, Fritz, let's go. I'm not alone. Fritz is Fritz's friend. I'm my own best friend.—All the things I should know. It's funny. But let's think about it all in the forest, what I could do to make my mother— (*Leaves quickly*.)

Room in MRS KOCHER*'s house.*
MRS KOCHER; ERNST, *her son, sitting in the armchair*; FRITZ.

MRS KOCHER. It's so nice of you to spend some time with my son, Fritz.

FRITZ. I really enjoy it.

ERNST. Wouldn't you rather play with the others? Wouldn't that be more fun?

FRITZ. No way. Sitting here quietly and talking to you is much more fun.

MRS KOCHER (*holding* FRITZ's *hand*). Where did they find such a beautiful soul? Someone so good inside.

FRITZ. You shouldn't praise me like that.

MRS KOCHER. It would be a crime not to. But I hear someone coming. Have fun. I'll be back with some dinner. A bit of wine and bread. Bye for now. (*She leaves*.)

FRITZ. You have a very nice mother.

ERNST. Oh, I can't say anything. What *can* you say?

FRITZ (*thoughtful*). Of course.

ERNST. It's so stupid. Why wouldn't a mother be nice and loving? I'm sure yours is too.

FRITZ. Not that I know.

ERNST. What?

FRITZ. I've never felt like I have a mother. On my backside, maybe.

ERNST. You're kidding?

FRITZ. How could I be kidding? There's nothing funny about it. I wish I were sick like you.

ERNST. I'm sure you would enjoy that.

FRITZ. More than you think. Listen!

ERNST. What?

FRITZ. Could you take a mother who doesn't love you? Would you care?

ERNST. What nonsense. A mother always loves her child. I'm sure yours loves you as well. You're just imagining things.

FRITZ (*upset*). Let's not talk about it any more.

Backyard. KLARA *and* PAUL.

KLARA. Where's Fritz?

PAUL. Oh, he said he's going to the pond, by the forest. He said—

KLARA. What did he say now?

PAUL. Nothing, really. He wants to drown himself.

KLARA (*frightened*). What?

PAUL. Well, yes. Life, he said, is nothing but a torn coat. He needs to mend it.

KLARA. What? Life is—

PAUL. I don't like to repeat myself. He wants to mend his life. He's tired of it. It's not worth anything. I forgot the rest.

KLARA. So go, go—

PAUL. Where?

KLARA. To the pond! I'm scared. You're still here? Why aren't you going?

PAUL. I'm not about to run my legs off because of that cursed life! It's not serious.

KLARA. And what if it is? Shame on you. He's our brother. If you don't want to go, then—

PAUL. Wait, I'm coming! (*Both leave.*)

A pond surrounded by evergreens. FRITZ *appears.*

FRITZ. How silent it is here. The trees reflected in the water. How it drips from the branches, so quiet, so delicate. You could mistake it for a song. The leaves are floating on the water like little boats. Here you could be properly sad and melancholy. But I didn't come here to cry. I need to get going. (*He takes off his coat.*) Right! I'll put this in the grass, over here. (*He throws his hat into the water.*) And the hat needs to learn how to swim. I told Paul that I'm tired of life, that I'm going to the pond. He understood. Truth is, it's time I get a bit of attention. Let's see if my mother is worried about me. Let's see if she's still indifferent when she hears that I jumped into the pond.—Paul should be here soon, and when he sees the hat and the coat, and I'm nowhere to be found, what else can he think? This has to work. I know it's bad to frighten your mother unnecessarily. But—I want to know whether she cares about me.—He's coming. I can hear him. That's his whistling. (*He climbs an evergreen. While climbing:*) I can't wait to see his face. He's going to take off. I already can't help laughing. (*He hides between the branches.*)

PAUL *appears, approaches the coat.*

PAUL. Oh, ah, there he is, there he is, in the grass. (*When he sees the empty coat and the hat in the water, he screams and runs away.*)

FRITZ *climbs down.*

FRITZ. Right. In ten minutes they'll know. Let's start walking home. I'm getting a bit scared myself. So what? What's the worst that can happen? Another thrashing? Same old story. How can I be afraid of something that I'm used to?—I don't even mind going the long way. It's only right if for once they're the ones running and crying. They ought to cry, and I'm happy about it. No one has ever cried because of me. Maybe now they'll see that I'm worth something. (*He uses a branch to retrieve his hat.*) This hat almost drowned. But I'm pleased with it; what a good job. Hat, you can sit back up. (*He puts it on his head.*) Right. Now I'll walk like a smug Englishman to the next forest. I feel very noble. The devil shall take me if I get home before evening.

Hallway.

KLARA, *crying, appears.*

KLARA. If he could just come home. Just come home! He couldn't have drowned. Who does something like that? Oh, why can't he just be back here? He can call me a stupid cow anytime he wants. A thousand times. Why was I always so mean to him? We weren't nice to him. Bad, bad. I can't even talk. I can't breathe. (*Frightened.*) Fritz, please come back. Can't you see that we're all crying because of you? The whole house is going mad. Please come back. I have to go. I can't stand still. It's black everywhere. I'm going to faint. Fritz, oh, Fritz. You bad, dear, stupid boy, oh—(*She lies on the ground and sobs.*)

FRITZ *appears.*

FRITZ. Here I am!—Hey, Klara! What are you doing on the ground?

KLARA (*yelling*). You? (*As if in a dream.*) You?

FRITZ. Yes! Why not?

KLARA. Didn't you jump into the water? Paul came home crying, said that you'd jumped into the pond!

FRITZ. Paul's a stupid boy.

KLARA. Didn't you tell Paul that you wanted to kill yourself? That life's a torn coat? That you wanted to get rid of it?

FRITZ (*defiantly*). And what if I did?

KLARA. Don't you realize that we've all been terribly worried? We searched all over for you.

FRITZ. So?

KLARA. Mother is beside herself. Yes, she's in there. I don't even dare go in there and tell her that you—

FRITZ. What?

KLARA. —that you're alive again. You have it coming, I tell you!

FRITZ. I don't care.

MRS MARTI *and* MR MARTI *appear.*

KLARA. Mama, Papa! Fritz didn't fall into the water. He doesn't have a spot of water on him.

FRITZ *stands there guilty and trembling.*

MR MARTI. Wha—you—

MRS MARTI (*trying to control herself, to her husband*). Leave him alone, Adolf. Don't hurt him, you hear?

MR MARTI. You trick us into thinking you're dead? That brat, that sluggard, that— (*He tries again to go after* FRITZ.)

MRS MARTI (*to her husband, firmly*). Leave him to me. I'll punish him. (*To* FRITZ, *concerned.*) Why did you do that?

FRITZ. I, I—I—

MRS MARTI. Why would you tell Paul that you want to throw yourself into the water? Why?

FRITZ. Mother, I—

MRS MARTI (*softly*). Come, let's go to the living room! Come! (*She takes him by the hand and leads him.*)

MR MARTI. His backside deserves a beating for this, the little bastard. This is what happens from sitting around doing nothing. We should take him out of school and put him in a factory. Nothing but playing tricks in his head. But I'll show him, that—(*He leaves, agitated.*)

KLARA. Oh, I'm just so glad he's back. He's got it really bad now. But they shouldn't punish him too much. I should go inside and listen to what they're saying. (*Listens at the door.*) I can't hear anything. It's silent. What does that mean? Is that Mother who's whispering—is it—someone's crying, but very softly. I don't get it. I don't get it.

The living room. MRS MARTI. FRITZ, *sitting half on her lap.*

MRS MARTI. But how can I know what's in your heart? I can't guess, can I? You should have said something. You have to speak when you want to say something. See, now I've done wrong to you. I thought you didn't love me, all you wanted to do was cause me grief. Oh, how wrong we can be about some things in this world. But it's fine now. Do say something.

FRITZ. I can't.

MRS MARTI. Why didn't you ever say anything? Why did you never tell me, Mother, you did me wrong—Mother, I love you—?

FRITZ. —love you—

MRS MARTI. And why not? Why suffer for no reason and not use your mouth? You poor boy!

FRITZ. I was never allowed to. A son can't do that.

MRS MARTI. But why not?

FRITZ. I thought you couldn't stand me, so I thought I better keep quiet. But you've always been my mother, and I've always loved you, in silence.

MRS MARTI (*kisses him*). Don't say that. (*She cries.*) Don't talk like that.

FRITZ. What else could I've done?

MRS MARTI. My boy, my boy, what are you doing to me? Do you want me to fall on my knees in front of you? Is that what you want?—Oh.—I've done you wrong, much wrong. But I'll make it up to you. We'll make it all better. What do you say? Everything's going to be fine, right? You and I will be like friends. A quiet, private alliance. Father doesn't need to know about it. Right?

FRITZ. No.

MRS MARTI. I'm not ashamed to be friends with you, since I now know what a strong lad you are. I now know that you're good. And you wouldn't listen less, or be less careful, because of it. You have to behave. And we as parents have to teach children to listen. But you know better than other children. We can talk to you in a different manner. You've had to suffer much. I've made you suffer much. You're already a big, big man. (*She smiles.*)

FRITZ (*snuggles up against her*). Mama!

MRS MARTI. I'm serious. But it's quite odd. I'm talking to you as if you were a grown person. Even though you're lying on me like this. On my lap! You, my child. My boy. I can't tell you how wonderful, how big you seem to me. I shouldn't have to say it. I'm more than happy to remain silent now. To be on my own for a little while. Go and see Klara, until we eat dinner. Go—

FRITZ. Yes, Mama. (*He wants to leave.*)

MRS MARTI. But wait. I must give you one more hug. You're not going to cause trouble with your sister and Paul because of this, right? I mean, because of how I've spoken to you? Right?

FRITZ. That would be mean.

MRS MARTI (*happy*). No, right? That would be a sin. A real sin. You won't do it, I know it. Go now.—(FRITZ *leaves.*) I hope I didn't go too far? (*Deeply moved.*) Did I go too far?—Can you speak to a child like this? No, no, that was fine. Something so beautiful can't possibly be bad. Should a mother always speak like a nun to her children? It had to be this way. Honesty can't do any harm. But is it different now between us? Doesn't he love me, and doesn't he have to keep listening to me, when he sees that I love him back? No, there's no trouble. I don't want to regret being honest. Just that would be very bad. Did someone see it? Nobody saw it, nobody would want to be seen. My son, I want to thank you, on my knees, for showing me.—Let me go now and see what they're doing.

The dining room. A lamp burns on the table. FRITZ, PAUL, KLARA *are playing.* MRS MARTI *stands in the dark and observes them.*

PAUL. So, this ink blot is the pond. Or not? This blot can't be the pond?

FRITZ. Of course it can. And I'm the knife.

KLARA. And what am I?

FRITZ. Wait, one thing after another. Watch, now the cheese knife is going after that black ink blot. No, the blot is going after the knife. No, just like this: The knife goes into this pond. That's the story. It's not the knife's fault. It's a very well-behaved knife.

KLARA. But it can't drown.

FRITZ. It doesn't really care much about that. And now, watch carefully, here comes the fork, running and jumping. Oh, how it plummets downward. And how it cries when it can't find the knife. How it just runs away. Who would've thought that a fork could have such legs.

PAUL. I was the fork.

KLARA. But what was I?

FRITZ. Just wait. It'll be your turn soon enough. As soon as the fork is gone, the knife emerges from the muddy water, cleans itself a bit and slowly walks home. At home, it sees the spoon on the ground. (*To* KLARA.) You're the spoon, if you want.

KLARA. It's true, you saw me on the ground when you came back.

FRITZ. It's difficult to describe the spoon's face.

KLARA. Did I make such a face?

FRITZ. You made about nine. You fell from one into the other. You could barely keep track of them, that's how fast your faces changed. That's what the spoon did. And now the story is over.

PAUL. What, I don't think so! Now there are two more people. Father appears and then Mother.

FRITZ. I don't know anything else. Let's use something else for a story.

They start something else.

MRS MARTI (*softly*). They didn't notice. I was right, and I will be right. He's acting the same. What a good boy. I can barely keep myself from going up to him, telling him.—Isn't it like a dream, a fairy tale? The lamp burns like a magic lamp. I stand like a fairy behind the children. The only thing missing is fairy-tale music. But you can always hear it in your ears. How lovely it all is. I must listen, oh how I must listen. Everything my children are saying seems so new today, so different. I've never heard them like this. And it's not like I just want to love my Fritz from now on. No, no, I love them all, and shall love them the same. Should they be?

Look how I tell myself. It's as if I'm my own pastor. What would the pastor accomplish with his talk if there wasn't already a pastor in all of us? So, I no longer want to be a spectator. (*Loudly*.) Children, what are you up to?

KLARA. We're making up stories, Mama. Fritz can tell beautiful stories.

MRS MARTI. Where does he get them all?

KLARA. Well, from his head. His head is a book full of stories. Now he's telling us one about a chambermaid.

PAUL. Where's Papa?

MRS MARTI. He'll be here soon. I think I can hear him already.—There he is.

MR MARTI *enters*.

MR MARTI (*gives* FRITZ *a strict look*). To bed, children, it's late.

MRS MARTI. No, not yet. Let's get a bottle of wine from the cellar. Let's stay up a bit longer and talk. Right, Adolf?—Yes, yes. Why not this once.

MR MARTI. Why not. Who's getting the wine?

FRITZ (*quickly*). I'll get it.

MRS MARTI (*as quickly*). I need to turn on the kitchen light for you. Come on!

MRS MARTI *and* MR MARTI *leave*. MR MARTI *packs his pipe*.

KLARA. Where are we in our story?

PAUL. Where they leave together to get some wine from the cellar.

PART II

The Early Dramolettes

THE BOYS

(1900)

A mountain pasture.

FRANZ, HERMANN, HEINRICH *appear.*

Far in the background, PETER, *as small as a rabbit.*

FRANZ. You no longer think of death when you have to climb like this. (*Throws himself onto the meadow.*)

HERMANN. Of course not, because your thoughts have no time to hatch something so sublime.

FRANZ. Have you thought of it often?

HERMANN. So often death seems nothing more than a dirty trick.

HEINRICH. You just never thought of trying it.

FRANZ. Heinrich is right. How charming it would be to try, taking on death. Go ahead and walk, balancing yourself across this fence, and you will feel it.

HEINRICH. Feel it?

FRANZ. Yes, 'Feeling is everything.'* O my Goethe! When will it be my time to play your Faust on stage? What bliss! All in glaring

* *Faust*, line 3456, which is followed by the rest of the famous quotation: 'Name is but echo and smoke'.

limelight, and then that still night of my spoken parts. Of course, you first must be able to speak.

HERMANN. So you are going into theatre?

HEINRICH. You want to exchange real life with its illusion, the body with its reflection?

FRANZ. Ah, the philosophers. I am going into the theatre with the intent of making my life there a vital one.

HEINRICH. Do it, do it, but isn't it hard?

FRANZ. It won't be very hard, for it will be easy enough once I come into my own.

HERMANN. Coming into one's own is often nothing but vanity.

FRANZ. Aren't you clever! Vanity is coming into one's own. If you are never vain about anything, then you will never conquer anything yourself. Ah, how beautiful it is here! What freedom! To just lie here and dream of greatness. (*He stands up.*) To walk around here and dream of greatness. (*He strolls to the back.*)

HEINRICH. Greatness?

HERMANN. He said greatness. Do you believe in it?

HEINRICH. I don't believe that I don't believe in it. Do I know? Do you know?

HERMANN. I don't know what greatness is.

HEINRICH. I know, but I cannot describe it. It is in my legs but not in my mouth.

HERMANN. Then I think it should be in my ears.

HEINRICH. Of course, you are a fiddler after all.

HERMANN. Don't speak like that—you're making fun of me.

HEINRICH. So make fun of me too.

HERMANN. I can't. I don't have the necessary intelligence or wit.

HEINRICH. You are a good chum. (*They fall silent.*)

HEINRICH. The sun will go down soon. Look how long the shadows are getting. They will soon touch us.

HERMANN. Is there anything more fragile than the lengthening of a shadow?

HEINRICH. Than being touched in such a way?

HERMANN. We are asking nature. We will never get an answer.

HEINRICH. But we will from our hearts.

HERMANN. Then we have to say a lot, explain, emphasize.

HEINRICH. No, you just need to remain silent, always.

HERMANN. Oh, you! (*They embrace.*)

HEINRICH. It's already touching your feet now.

HERMANN. What? Ah, the shadow.

HEINRICH. What is the meaning of a shadow?

HERMANN. Death, life? Greatness? Silence?

HEINRICH. We must stop asking these questions. You cannot ask so many questions out loud. It will divide us. To quarrel with you would be death. I have never liked anyone as much as I like you.

HERMANN. I don't know what it is, but with the girls it all seems so empty, so loveless.

HEINRICH. I wouldn't know.

FRANZ *returns. The others.*

HEINRICH. Well? Have you finished dreaming of your greatness? Are you so small-minded that you would rejoin us?

FRANZ. One does get tired of dreaming.

HERMANN. Dreaming is like rain, it softens so.

FRANZ. No, dreaming is like the evening sun, sweet and red, but hard and painful.

HEINRICH. Is it hurting you?

FRANZ. When I left you my dreaming was as bright as noontime, it went deep into my soul and returned like new. Now it is damaged, torn, deformed, apart—it is like night. *That* hurts—am I not right, pageboy?

HEINRICH. Don't remind me of that.

FRANZ. But listen, listen, you dark cliffs, you wicked figures of nature: Over there is a page. He is pale with love for his mistress. His mistress is a fat wench. Her hair is red, her mouth is swollen, her chin is double, her gait is clumsy and her eyes are lead.

HEINRICH. Be still—I have no such mistress.

FRANZ (*laughing wildly*). Shall I describe another one? Perhaps she will do?

HEINRICH. No, describe nothing but a boundary for your unrestrained mind, such that it cannot slip out.

HERMANN. Shouldn't we go home?

FRANZ (*suddenly serious*). Go home?

HERMANN. I'm getting too cold here. I need to keep moving. Where is Peter?

HEINRICH. He did come with us.

FRANZ. Yes, he is probably somewhere pealing turnips or eating grass. Come on, let's go.

HERMANN. Peter, Peter! Hey, Peter! (*They exit.*)

Late evening. PETER *steps forward.*

PETER. They are calling me. They shout my name with such cockiness. They will go home without me. Perhaps they are angry, lacking a subject for their amusement on the way back. I am usually the subject. What a terribly ridiculous figure I am to them. I am forever the cause of their laughter. Even my anger is funny to them, to the fiddler, the actor, the pageboy. I am without title, without talent, unless crying counts as one. I am a gifted crier. I do cry with talent, but this is not art in the eyes of an artist. Because it is not art. (*He smiles.*) No, not art, because it comes only from the heart. (*He lies on the ground.*)

Night chased them away, but she is used to me. I am night's darling. Shouldn't I be loved by something, too? But it is sad: I'm loved only by her. She is all black, I can see that. All moist, I can feel that. Good-hearted, I know that. It is up to me to paint her profound charms in even more detail. I am a painter. My tears are my oils, which I mix with my colours, and these are my feelings. I paint with feelings, and they are sighing, lamenting, longing. Longing is the hottest of my colours. My colours often run into a big lake—love. I must always, always love. Others might put it away neatly at times, but I cannot. Then there comes a night, like today, like this one, and I am all love, tears, longing, filthiness. (*His head on the ground, he cries audibly.*)

I suppose all this loving (*He props up his head.*) will have to end at some point, but then my life would end, that is certain.

My love for life is nothing more than the love I have for my mother, and she is dead. They didn't lower her into the earth, they threw her. She was a despised yet beautiful woman. My love falls after her, totally ridiculous, totally desperate. She was a poor but beautiful woman. Her beauty, which was more than beauty, pulls me down to where she was thrown, not lowered. But I don't hate the people for what they have done.

There is no reason to hate the deceived, and the people who threw my mother have been deceived. They will never discover the secret of beauty. I am, however, more than willing to die in order to discover the secret of beauty. (*He cheers up.*)

If I want to die this young, such is the joy of sleep. Youth enjoys sleep because it tires easily. And I am so blissfully tired. You are used to letting fatigue sadden you. But it makes me happy. It promises so much, it promises death. A kiss from my mother. I love to be dead tired, so that it reminds me of her kiss. I cannot have the kiss without death. So, because the kiss is so dear to me, death is, too. Death kisses me. I wish it would. I wish it would. I wish it would. (*Sad, he exits.*)

Change of scene.
An empty street. FRANZ *and* HERMANN *appear.*

HERMANN. What did the actor Jank* say to you?

FRANZ. That I didn't have any talent, that I'm missing the divine spark.

HERMANN. What is that?

FRANZ. Talent. Let me explain it to you in more detail. He asked me to recite a poem or a speech.

* Walser may have borrowed the name from the famous scene painter and stage designer Christian Jank (1833–88). Walser's older brother Karl was a scene painter.

HERMANN. And you were brilliant at it.

FRANZ. I was not brilliant, for that thespian's face passed into a worried smile during my recitation, whereby he consoled one for his lack of talent.

HERMANN. And you accepted it and left?

FRANZ. First, the divine spark was explained to me. Then it was explained that I take my leave of a stage career for the swindle that it is. He had fine lips, a stern voice, noble manners, an upright posture, a serenity to his movements, a genteel demeanour and what one might call a gesture which fit him perfectly. But all this became incredible to me, I nearly wept. And then the great, kind man said: My dear boy, there is no helping it, you lack the divine spark.

HERMANN. And so you left?

FRANZ. No, for I had to listen to the divine spark being once more unwrapped and revealed. I felt sick, and if art is about this spark, then I want nothing to do with it.

HERMANN. Do you want to hear how I fared with Paganini?

FRANZ. Do tell, tell!

HERMANN. First I shall begin with a spindly thin man, for that was my first impression of the master, and all he had to show. Then he extended his hand, so thin, so thin. Upon this he measured me with his eyes—I felt stabbed. Then he asked me to play a piece—his voice was the most tender song, and the opening of his lips nothing but strokes of the bow. I played and earned little approval, his indignant displeasure if anything, for the master said with his head only 'No'. I tell you, a weary, bored 'No'. I didn't know how to respond, so I put away my violin and left, and now—I am done playing the violin.

FRANZ. You're right, if finding a master means enduring such martyrdom.

HERMANN. Let's give up everything.

FRANZ. I will go to war. France is recruiting soldiers.

HERMANN. I have a bit of money, but nothing else. I will come with you.

FRANZ. Heinrich will join us as well, unless he fares far better with his lady than we did with art.

HERMANN. Here they come.

FRANZ. Oh for heaven's sake, hide. (*They hide.*)

The noble LADY, HEINRICH.

HEINRICH.

You most beautiful of women,
covered only by a sweet dress.
I'm your prisoner, yours alone.
Lost I but am because of you,
because of your sublime beauty.
O please appoint me as your page,
the train-bearer of your troubles.
Even if there's no train at all,
you still offer plenty to bear,
you who are all sacred to me.
O turn your head towards where I am.
O just look at me with a smile,
and dub me your faithful page,
who's so in love with servitude.
To serve you is sheer bliss to me,
it is to savour beauty's stem,
because you are sweet beauty's tree.

LADY.

What is it you wish, my young man?
To serve me, well, that's very nice.
You seem to be very well taught,
to flatter for flattery's art.
You seem rather charming as well,
and gladly my eyes dwell on you,
one so faithful in appearance.
Save the test of faith is wanting,
but this want shall not count for much.

HEINRICH.

O sweet voice, echo on and on,
my ears have yet to feel content.

FRANZ.

O this is delicious. This will be a joke for months to come.

HERMANN.

They're speaking in verse, listen.

HEINRICH.

To serve you, your lovely body
to feel, O you dearest woman.

LADY.

You must never forget yourself.
That said, I have this strong desire
to take you with me after all,
to measure you for your costume.

HEINRICH.

O permit me to kiss your hand,
those fingers of yours, whose smoothness
makes me so happy, as it must
be so happily fitting at last.

LADY.

If you wish to be a sweet boy,
practise kissing your own fingers,
for you cannot be so tender
or gentle enough in such things.

HEINRICH.

Please forgive me. My being in love
is not yet used to metes and bounds.

They exit.

FRANZ. The way he kissed her hand. Excellent.

HERMANN. What a clown. Here he comes again. (*He bows.*) 'O permit me to kiss your hand.'

Those above. HEINRICH.

FRANZ. What? Heinrich. You leave so quickly the place that carried you away?

HERMANN. You were pulling some funny faces. We saw it all, it was like the theatre.

FRANZ. You were speaking in verse. Disgusting.

HEINRICH. She left me standing there.

FRANZ. She laughed at you?

HEINRICH. She just disappeared. I was so delighted to look at her, to think of her.

FRANZ. And then she slipped through a street door.

HEINRICH. I don't know.

HERMANN. Didn't she say that she disliked your sighing?

FRANZ. That your behaviour was childish?

HEINRICH. She didn't say anything like it.

FRANZ. She should have said for the sake of your saving face. Look: We are joining the army. Art is a waste of time. The warrior is far above it. This will be the last thing I undertake, but I will do so as a man.

HERMANN. I have slain my weakness. I have become a man.

FRANZ. All three of us will be men.

HEINRICH. Me too.

FRANZ. Wait, what about Peter?

HEINRICH. Yes, Peter.

HERMANN. Peter must stay with us. Of course! This way we will never stop laughing.

FRANZ. Where is he?

HERMANN. I saw him sitting in some corner, like a beetle. He was staring into space. His hand fell over his head like a willow tree. He got clubbed.

FRANZ. Well, he should be a club himself.

HEINRICH. We will use him for a club on others.

FRANZ. Whatever. Let's go. (*All exit.*)

Change of scene.
A forest. PETER *appears through the trees.*

PETER. They wanted me to come along. I kept saying no. It went on like this for an hour. At last they accepted my stubbornness. And now it is time to die. My dream is coming true. All is set here, the place and hour of my fulfillment. How beautiful it is in the forest. I hear the loveliest music, the most faithful spoken parts, the most honest yearning. My crying stops. What is this I cannot cry? I know why. I can't say why. It simply brings me joy. I have earned this life through weeping. Death comes free of charge. I have paid nothing for the best as I paid richly for the grief, the disloyalty, the ignorance. I was always getting beaten, but now Heaven opens its eyes for me. It has enormously wide eyes. Well, this is how I will die. I can do it before my time, because I am already so tired. There is still much to say that is inexpressible. Surely we can speak the unspeakable. But the fir trees are so still they demand silence, death. Because my mother was so dear to me, I die. (*He dies.*)

The wind rustles in the trees.
Peter's mother enters with outstretched arms, rushing towards him.

POETS

(1901)

A street. A house on the left, a garden on the right.

SEBASTIAN.

SEBASTIAN. I will sit down on this old house's stone bench. Nobody is around whom I could tell how tired I am. I am a poet. It is my calling to coax feelings into meagre rows of syllables we call poetry. My poems are judged by the shrugs and cool glances of those who read them, quite poorly, I might add. But I am not complaining, that is for sure. There is nothing you can do about it. My lamenting, no matter how moving it might be, is not capable of making me a better artist. I force myself to keep writing. That is what many other poets do, and they are being forced, if anything, by plenty of rather horrendous reasons. Perhaps what really spurs me on is simply the sheer boredom of writing about things that look back at me through the words and cause me sorrow, if not something worse. The world just brushes it all aside. Half-talents such as me, it seems, are a joke to her. She accepts what she ought to vigorously reject. She does call me a fool—it is just that I am not foolish enough. But she would not dare tell me to my face. I get it from behind, from the side, through whispers from above. The world keeps reminding me. Oh, if only I had a calling to earn my bread more honestly than this half of one in which I am three-quarter stuck. Is that not Hermann?

HERMANN *appears*.

HERMANN. Laugh, laugh!

SEBASTIAN. Well, what is it?

HERMANN. Kaspar has hanged himself! The famous Kaspar. He whose naked shoulders were just now being caressed by golden fame. The critics' darling, as they say, worshipped by women, flooded with praise. My mouth cannot even spit it out.

SEBASTIAN. And he has just hanged himself, this moment?

HERMANN. He could not take the fame.

SEBASTIAN. Did it not suit him?

HERMANN. In a way, yes. He wore it like the beggar who wears the king's robe, sighing and walking with a stoop. His shy, clumsy, diffident, pondering figure soon shed itself of what it was not called to wear. The silk, the pearls, the precious objects of fame were hurting him. Such people are not made for the smell of roses and the chink of gold.

SEBASTIAN. His desire for things forbidden made for such sweet poetry.

HERMANN. He was right to leave us in the dust: That thought was a fine inspiration. His name, his name! If only I could be a letter in his name.

SEBASTIAN. It would be a great help to me if I were simply its sound. I would be swimming in the ether and soaking in my own echo.

HERMANN. We are the tongues that speak his name. The entire world is doing the same at this moment. How it loves the name of a dead celebrity. Gabriel, that jolly Gabriel, you hear, should give the eulogy. There is talk of a marvellous funeral.

SEBASTIAN. You think they would know what to do with the dead poet. After all, they let him starve when he was still alive.

HERMANN. I understand. They made him famous but never offered him a hand, a hand the love-craving poet would have loved to grab. They moved into the background in order to shout even louder. They wear fine clothes, stroll with cultured ladies, hold spirited conversations, love the extraordinary because it nourishes their wits. Woe to the outsider who dares to join their circle, where they smile at each other in boredom. You are coming, too, right?

SEBASTIAN. Where? Ah! To master Gabriel!

HERMANN. Let us hear how far his thundering voice can reach.

SEBASTIAN. Where will he be giving his speech?

HERMANN. On the steps of the town hall. There will be plenty of people and tears for Kaspar. His name will have to help them sweeten the moist night air.

SEBASTIAN. Tomorrow night? I will be there!

HERMANN. Let us go. (*They leave.*)

A window opens above. OSKAR *leans out.*

OSKAR. I do not know how many times I have stuck my head out of the window at this hour. It is the same every night. I cannot account for it. I contemplate the stars and find something floating above their beauty, something I cannot explain. The moon kisses the vast world and the silent spot here in front of the house. The trees lisp. The fountain shivers. My ears are much too sensitive for night's laughter. I think I have been writing poems for the past few days without even knowing why. My back is breaking because of it, because for hours I bend over a word, waiting for its long journey from brain to paper. And I feel neither miserable nor happy. I simply forget myself. The number of poems I have written can be counted on one hand, that is, if I were bothered enough to count them. What would be the point? Something tells me that I will die doing it. The beauty of the stars, the moon, the night and the trees torments me. It does not offer any peace to the one who trembles. In the past, I would sit by the window as often and long as I do now but without feeling the slightest stirring of emotions. My head is aching from all this brooding. My feelings are arrowheads wounding me. My heart longs to be wounded. My thoughts long to be weary. I want to press the moon into a poem and the stars into another and add myself between them. What else shall I do with these feelings but let them die like flapping fish on the sands of language? The end of my poetry will be the end of me, and I welcome it, happily. Good night!

Change of scene. Town-hall square.
On a frame draped in black silk, Kaspar's coffin. Torches.
GABRIEL, SEBASTIAN, HERMANN *and others.*

SEBASTIAN. I should think your voice will drum up enough people.

HERMANN. And if not, a pair of ears more or less will not matter here.

GABRIEL. Shortly, shortly.

SEBASTIAN. You should trample their ears all the same.

HERMANN. I have yet to hear your voice.

SEBASTIAN. He will make you feel it. Now, Gabriel, our impatience urges you to begin.

GABRIEL. In a moment. (*He climbs the steps up to the coffin.*) Ladies and gentlemen! Gracious assembly! A few poets have invited me to speak at today's funeral for Kaspar. Even without such a reminder, for which I am honoured, I would never have found it in me not to be vocal here. Whatever I say comes from the heart, so there can be no talk of a rousing, beautiful funeral address. Kaspar was very dear to me. I admired him. I am grieved, and I weep for him. His life was short but radiant and glorious. As soon as the angel of fame's kiss arrived, the angel of death was ready to collect him. And I do not gain anything by mentioning his premature fame. The world made it clear that admiration lay at his feet. His poems, whose euphony rattled our ears, will be his marble monument at whose red-stained pedestal* we will weep. He is at peace now. My speech shall not be long. (*He descends.*)

SEBASTIAN. Well done, well said, extremely well timed.

HERMANN. His voice is still roaring in my ears.

SEBASTIAN. Let's shake his hand.

HERMANN. Let's shake him off with a brave handshake.

SEBASTIAN. I wanted to be Kaspar's name.

* A rhetorical prop employed to describe political assassinations, such as the blood-stained pedestal of Pompeii in Gérôme's *César mort*.

Change of scene. In front of the POETESS' *house.*

POETESS. What a beautiful morning. The weary soul can rest comfortably in this cool air, this invigorating breeze. The dream loses itself. I had one, if not absurd then certainly most strange. I stood there musing with a goose quill in my hand. Suddenly a handsome and slender young man began kissing my hand, spurred by the most heated and unbridled adoration for me. I do not remember how many times his red lips, which smiled at me like the pages of an open book, kissed my pale hands, which grew paler with each passionate and moist touch. I became quite hot, and I have every reason to still be in fever when I think of what is about to happen next. For the dream threw out an entire forest of young men from within itself, all of whom crowded around my smiling condescension, kissing whatever sweet thing there was to kiss. They flew, swarmed and worshipped around me like bees buzzing around a hive or soldiers surrounding their victorious general. Neither their kissing nor their cooing and stammering ever ceased. Some pleaded, others wept. One of them, probably the most exuberant, was laughing like one possessed. His laughter kissed me as much as everything else. They all had such red, fresh, seductive lips, like the pages of an open book. What a dream! What material for a novella. What a lovely feeling to be kissed all over again by the vitality of these images! It looks like nothing will come of my resolution to write ten to twelve poems today. That said, I by no means want to trade the pleasure of this dream with this respite, the drafting and dispatching of a novella and a half. O those young men! I shall return to the house and continue to delight in them. (*She enters the house.*)

SEBASTIAN, GABRIEL, HERMANN *arrive*.

SEBASTIAN. Is this her house?

GABRIEL. You don't want to go in, do you?

HERMANN. She will stab you to death with the tips of her virginal moustache.

SEBASTIAN. I am going in, whatever the cost.

HERMANN. We will all go in.

GABRIEL. We will examine her. We will whisper sweetly into the eager ears of the authoress' vanity.

SEBASTIAN. We will make her turn red.

HERMANN. I can but promise little satisfaction from this. But so be it. And I will speak to her in verse.

SEBASTIAN. Gabriel's voice shall shout for forgiveness.

GABRIEL. She will sense the true enthusiasm behind our visit and welcome us as poets.

SEBASTIAN. She will speak of Kaspar like some sad wretch for whom it was time to go.

HERMANN. That's when I will pull her by the ears.

GABRIEL. You will first have to entreat her forlorn, somewhat barbed and acid dignity for permission.

SEBASTIAN. I will say I would, if I may . . .

GABRIEL. And she will say: Calm yourself, sir. Please, no noise. My house has until now been a refuge for decent people. And even then only as an exception.

HERMANN. An unfortunate exception, that is what I will call her.

GABRIEL. I can already see that our visit is falling overboard.

SEBASTIAN. No, he should stick his finger into the fire and see what burning tastes like.

GABRIEL. My heart, my lady, my sweet, sweet . . .

HERMANN. A glorious voice! Keep going! Go inside so we can get out.

GABRIEL. The thought of getting out of here will be a pleasure, once we are really inside, that is.

SEBASTIAN. Inside, voice.

HERMANN. Inside, sweet nerves.

GABRIEL. Inside, scoundrels.

Change of scene. The street from the first scene. The house on the left, the garden on the right. SEBASTIAN.

SEBASTIAN. I am weary of my reproaches, which I have been doing to myself for some time now. Why should I not be good at something an honest person is not: Being a fool? We call each other fools, but nobody knows the real fool, for the real fool is in all of us. Is Gabriel a fool? Certainly! Is Hermann a fool? No less, for sure! We want to be lied to, and when we speak the truth, it is only out of fear of lying. The coward lies the most. However, I am tired of foolish, fraudulent self-reproach, much like any other bad habit. I want to look at this gay fountain in peace and think that whatever creature comes forth maundering and rotting is composed of two bodies and four legs but only half a mind. Here it is as beautiful as in a fairy tale.

HERMANN *and* GABRIEL *appear.*

GABRIEL. I felt like I had to meet you here, only here and nowhere else in the world.

HERMANN. We heard you say it is as beautiful as a fairy tale here.

SEBASTIAN. The fountain is tittering at that tired, time-served wit of yours. Make it better, once you get the feeling back.

HERMANN. Such I have, but I am unable to guarantee you this, as my tongue disdains it.

GABRIEL. Have you read the lead story in today's morning paper?

SEBASTIAN. I do not read newspapers. I am too sensitive for it.

HERMANN. But this lead story, which is about Kaspar, should just about cure you of your sensitivity.

SEBASTIAN. I will read it. Here it is, as beautiful as a fairy tale.

GABRIEL. The clouds drift, the trees shiver, the air trembles, the stars flicker, the moon burns, and the most beautiful thing is this clever water jet over there, splashing the leaves.

HERMANN. I am tired.

GABRIEL. Of poetry?

HERMANN. Yes. Tell me, where is a poet's home?

GABRIEL. In time, in memory, in oblivion.

SEBASTIAN. In the grace offered to us by furtive spirits.

HERMANN. So our home is a gift of spirits. We live in the palace of the princess of spirits.

SEBASTIAN. Are you feeling calm now?

HERMANN. Oh, yes. I shall break out of myself. My thoughts cannot be my master.

GABRIEL. Listen, listen. Is that not a voice?

HERMANN. A bright voice, by Jove!

SEBASTIAN. Hush, hush!

OSKAR (*leaning out of the window*). I want to release my thoughts like canaries from a caged mind that is much too small. They shall fill this sacred, sweet night with enchanting chirping. My voice shall call after them: Go on, go on, do not ever return to me. Use the beautiful freedom I am giving you and grant me peace. But there are leftover feelings with which I cannot deal. I want to scatter them in the world's dark space, so they get stuck like stars. Fickle feelings that stray in our hearts have much in common with the flickering of stars. The night will not mind if I enrich it with such glowing symbols, feelings. The world wants me in its space, and I am close to dissolving in her embrace. What is going on down there? Hey?

SEBASTIAN. What is the matter with this fellow?

HERMANN. Let him be! He is dreaming. He is a poet. His voice is magnificent.

GABRIEL. I have nothing against his voice.

OSKAR (*up by the window*). When I disperse, I want to scream. It shall resound through a million valleys and over a million mountains. The night will weep. The earth will rotate more furiously, and people will feel that poets do not die alone.

PART III

Fairy Tales

CINDERELLA

(1901)

A garden behind a house.

CINDERELLA.

I will not cry so that they scream
at me for crying. My crying,
not their screaming, is what's awful.
When their hate doesn't make me cry,
the hate is good and sweet as cake.
It would be a jealous black cloud
blotting out the sun if I cried.
No, if I cried, I'd feel the hate
so hard it wouldn't be content
with mere tears. It would take my life,
that monster would eat me to death.
Its highly poisonous nature
is so lovely to me, the blithe
creature who never cries, who knows
no tears save only those of joy,
of only mindless happiness.
There is an imp inside my head
and he knows nothing of sadness.

Whenever they make me cry, there
cries this mirthfulness inside me.
When they hate me, my joy loves them
that cannot even hate the hate.
When they come for me blind with rage,
with poison arrows of their wrath,
I smile like so. My presence shines
like the sun to theirs. Its bright ray
may not touch them, but in a flash
it will dazzle their wicked hearts.
And I, since I'm always occupied,
I really have no time for crying,
only laughter! Work laughs. Hands laugh.
They do. This soul laughs with a joy,
with what should win over the souls
of others no matter how stubborn.
Come heart, laugh my troubles away.

She wants to go. Her sister, in the window above.

FIRST SISTER.

That thing acts as though she were worth
looking at, standing there stock-still,
like a pillar in the sunlight,
splendour to the eye only she sees.
Get your lazy hide to the kitchen.
Do you no longer remember
your scant responsibilities?

CINDERELLA.

I'm going already, calm yourself.
Some reverie overtook me

as I was on my way just now.
I was thinking of how pretty
you are, your darling sister too,
how you wear such pretty faces,
how it makes me more envious.
Forgive me and let me humbly
take my leave now.

She exits.

FIRST SISTER.

What a silly stupid dreamer.
We're far too soft on her. The fake
secretly laughs us off, pulling
a sad face when we surprise her
laughing at us behind our backs.
From now on, I'll give her the whip
for being so lazy on the sly.
That apron wraps her up in such
a dusty, black cloud. Then she dreams
about beauty, the hypocrite,
she who loafs even now. I'll go
and see that she gets back to work.

She closes the window.
Change of scene.
A room in the royal palace.

PRINCE.

What makes me so melancholy?
Is my mind taking leave of me?
Is my life oppressed by remorse?
Is it in my nature to grieve?

Grief is sweet joy's adversary,
which I feel when I'm miserable.
But from where comes this specious shame
oppressing my forsaken wits?
Neither one's mind can tell me why,
nor its companion, one's insight.
I simply bear it in silence
while it weighs on me.—Ah, music!*
Whose voice sounds so serenely clear?
Whatever it is, I kiss it
kissing me so impossibly.
In this sweet kiss lies tranquil calm.
Grief has fled. I hear nothing more
than this sound. I feel nothing more
than this lovely dance's lesson
with my limbs. Could melancholy
dance with so light a step? Well, there,
it's flown out of the door and I feel
wonderfully happy once more.
The Fool?

FOOL.

It's the Fool indeed and ever
the fool, it's the fool of the realm,
the world's fool and that dear sweet fool
who'd be nothing if not foolish,
the paragon of foolery,
a fool on Monday and likewise
Saturday night, a fool all told,

* Cinderella's singing.

a fool for himself and for his lord,
a right humble fool for his lord.

PRINCE.

Now tell me something: What is grief?

FOOL.

It is a fool, and who admits
it himself is no less a fool.
That you are its fool I can tell
by that bittersweet face of yours.
Oy, even your youth calls you fool
and so happens the fool himself.

PRINCE.

Is there not a cause for my grief?

FOOL.

You are its cause, the soil from which
it gaily blooms. You are the scales
on which it weighs itself, the bed
on which it lies stretched out. There is
no other reason save yourself.

PRINCE.

How then can I escape this grief
when I am such a pool of it,
what I would dare call: Grief itself?

FOOL.

Does a fool have to tell you this?
Should foolishness be so lofty,
may I ask, over the head of
a well-bred man? Why? Admit it,
this thing ill suits that wit of yours.

PRINCE.

I have whipped my wit, I flog it
like a tired lazy dog no more.
Now it's dead and it will never
wag its little tail any more.

FOOL.

I think it's right that we switch clothes.
You are a fool and as a fool
I take you by the ear. Next slap
yourself on the head, call yourself
stupid, and then stoop low
to my jokes which ridicule you.
Is this what you want? Have you had
enough of majesty—really?

PRINCE.

I'd be happy to give them up.
However, for your cap and bells,
I cannot exchange my burden,
which I would gladly throw away.

FOOL.

Go hunting. A spirited steed,
the exultant call of the horns—
such glories this vocation has,
to slay the thing which you mean here,
inconsolable grief, that is.

PRINCE.

Very well, I take your counsel
no more, no less than my father
takes his from his wise chancellor

when his own wisdom seems lacking.
Come, follow me. I shall exit
this scene like an old-fashioned prince
in a classic play. Today, Fool,
you are a fool in the best sense.

He exits.

FOOL.

By the devil, that I can believe,
and for me it would be easy.
It doesn't lack in flattery.
At heart, I am very flattered.
A prince well proves himself a fool
taking care not to be a fool.
I, who am not a prince, am lord
in the proper sense of the word,
for I am a master of wit.
My wit prevails over my lord,
who fell from his wit as my wit
raised him up to his princely state.
A prince with no fool is that wit
which will flop over and over.
I am buffoonery enthroned
above his station and scorning
a prince so in need of his fool.
And thus am I his fool indeed,
that I am for his foolishness.
Come, Fool, and let's follow the fool.

He exits.
Change of scene.

*An avalanche in the forest.** PRINCE *on horseback.*

PRINCE.

Down into the plain and raging,
like a storm-swollen stream. Trees fall
before my eyes. The heavens reel.
The world's a joyous chase, a game
preserve for noble hunters whose
minds range above earthly pursuits.
What cheer I feel, what sweet pluck,
how happy I am. This courage
makes my heavy soul feel light,
like a bird feels on the wing.
Right now, I feel like a painting—
lifeless, and yet so full of life,
fully in control, yet excited,
bitter and sweet. This carefree chase
is, indeed, the very image
of noble courage which I serve now
with all my heart while forgetting
what's so heartfelt. The forest is
my passion. It is my ballroom
where arms and legs feel joyfully
exercised. The trees are the rugs
and pillows at my father's court.
How wonderfully they wrap me.
No dream could be more beautiful.
No picture sweeter than this art
a benevolent goddess painted herself.

* An ironic play on teichoscopy, a classic dramatic device.

Today was time spent like a warrior,
a moment so exquisitely fulfilled.
It's a joy that goes by all too soon.

Change of scene.
A large room with a gallery connected by a flight of stairs.
CINDERELLA *and* FIRST SISTER.

CINDERELLA.

Look down at my devotion.
Look, look. O my every feeling
is ready to be at your service.
It is like a dress-shop box
opened to show a gift within,
like a new fur to keep you warm.
O how warmly my heart serves you.
I beg you, boldly slap my hand
if I should even for a second,
so long as the bat of your eye,
tarry in my duty. That can
never be, for my duty
is my only, my sweetest joy.

FIRST SISTER.

You stupid kitchen wench, not worth
the flogging you'd get from the whip.

CINDERELLA.

I'm always at your feet. I could
kiss your hand, that gentle hand,
the one which never strikes me
save for rightful punishment.
With your eyes, you regard me

like the sun. And I am the soil
which thrives on its merciful kiss,
on which nothing else ever can
as it lovingly blooms to you.
But, alas, loving I am not.
Indeed, I am devoid of love—
only my sister is the fairest,
yet not so beautiful as kind.
She is prettier than kindness.
What joy there to be at her feet,
to be her devoted servant.

FIRST SISTER.

Stop prattling so much. The time spent
talking could be spent doing some work,
putting forth devoted effort.
Now take your hand off my dress!

CINDERELLA.

If I must serve devotedly
and I mustn't require a hand,
with what shall I do my work?
Would it only get done in thoughts
on the fly, then this filthy hand
that angers you won't be required.
My yearning would put on your clothes,
wait on you with the finest things.
Then my heart would be a servant,
one just gentle enough, perhaps.
So a joy for work works for you—
would that not also work for you?

FIRST SISTER.

Would you shut up for once. And who
likes hearing all this chatter too.

CINDERELLA.

And who would—indeed—and my tongue
must work in a hurry with my hand
such that happiness keeps them both
out of breath. This way, when a word
leaps out of my mouth and would tempt
my hand, when it lures from the tongue
its abundance, my merry words
soon double what my hands do, like
words with fingers. Hand and voice kiss,
both married in the dearest way.

FIRST SISTER.

Both of them are lazy. And you,
their mistress, are as well. That's why
you must forever be beaten.
Off with you now.

She exits.

CINDERELLA (*calling to her*).

Beat me, beat me.

PRINCE *appears above in the gallery.*

PRINCE.

I don't know how I came into
this fairy tale. I only asked
for a drink the way hunters do.
However, these rooms here are such
the eyes can't see, the mind not easily

grasp. A glow floats upon the wall.
The scent of yellow roses spreads forth.
Like a soul it comes and goes
and solemnly takes my hand.
I stand still as if enchanted.
This thing clings to my senses.
Then this narrow space reopens.
The roof sways. This gallery dances
softly underfoot. What's going on?
Ah, below is some sweet presence.
I will accept what this thing is
even if I can't understand it.

CINDERELLA.

Whichever way or direction,
I'm spun around in a circle,
making my behaviour all wrong,
and this heart a ball for a game!
Feelings roll just like little balls,
going this way and that for fun.
I, she who should be stopping them,
I am the object of this game.
This scares me, at the same time
I've so little to fret over.
I laugh, yet in my laughter
something's serious, ominous
which makes me laugh blissful once more.
The seriousness in my toil
is such frightening fun, it would make
even bitter fate smile, something
I would think is quite difficult.

No, whenever I cried, my cares
and troubles laughed at me. I would
much rather laugh them both away
to poignant and beloved things.
There is still plenty of time left
to cry once time itself has cried.

PRINCE (*leaning over the railing*).

Are you a fairy tale, fair child?
Are your feet, are your hands too such
that if I touched them their beauty
would disappear into thin air?
I beg of you as one who pleads
for mercy. Are you an image,
and only appear as such? Speak!

CINDERELLA.

My lord! I am Cinderella.
See the dirt on my dress? It says
so as clearly as does my mouth.

PRINCE.

You are an angel. Tenderness,
as though embarrassed by that word's
meaning, stammers you're an angel.
What else could you be?

CINDERELLA.

A rather false and foolish thing,
who would like to know who you are.

PRINCE.

You give and receive my answer
at the very same time you ask.

CINDERELLA.

No, don't tell me. You are a prince,
son of a king. This I can see
in this lost creature no longer
fitting our time. An ermine cape
has been draped over your shoulders.
You wear a sword and hold a spear
out of fashion. That's what I think,
although I could be mistaken.
A king's son, surely you are.

PRINCE.

Surely, just as you are to me
a bride.

CINDERELLA.

Did you say that I am your bride?
O don't say that! It hurts to be
mocked and so tenderly misloved
by such a well-meaning young man.

PRINCE.

I can already see a crown
shimmering, pressed into your hair,
an image before which art stands
aloof and love looks at a loss.

CINDERELLA.

Why did you come here then and how?

PRINCE.

This the fairy tale tells you last,
when on the dear fairy tale's lips
this silence lies, when voice and sound,

colour and din and waterfall
and lake and forest have faded.
When this happens, at once just how
will spring into your eyes. But then
why I am here I do not know.
Pity and tenderness indeed
are furtive spirits, whose work can't
be divined. So simply be still.
Submit yourself to the stern fate
which has befallen you. It will
all come to an explanation.

CINDERELLA *falls into contemplative sleep.*
KING *and* CHANCELLOR *appear above in the gallery.*

KING.
Look, we have snared the griffin bird.*
Now have I got my claws on you,
you rascal, you good-for-nothing.
That it's my son makes me angry.

PRINCE.
Hush, Father, don't trouble yourself.

KING.
I am not troubled by this son,
who stands there like a red-faced boy
at my reproach. Are you facing
some knave, me who came upon you,
that you dare speak in such a way?
Explain to the high crown right now

* A mildly pejorative expression in the German, compare to a 'rare' or 'strange bird'.

how you came here, right here, here and
now. Spit it out! Hey! Will I get
this stammering confession soon,
which runs circles round my ears?

PRINCE.

I neither wear a red face, nor
would I stammer as you believe.
Calm yourself down, Father, be still.
I have an announcement to make,
to you, the realm, the world: I am
engaged.

KING.

How so?

PRINCE.

Yes, yes, engaged in every sense,
as one's words can only convey,
a vow to pledge, so I'm engaged.

KING.

Well! To whom?

PRINCE.

To a miracle who will not
be a miracle. A creature
such that only a girl can be,
yet like a girl unheard of.
An image before whom magic
takes a knee and rubs its blind eyes.
The divine thing's in the picture,
so it moves, has life and belongs

to me as I to it. It's a bond,
my father, not to be broken.
Blood was shared, and in ours no one
will see the sweetest love end.

KING.

Come, Chancellor, come!

PRINCE.

Allow me to kiss your hand, let
love fall down and beg at your feet.
She's the one I want to be mine,
who's worth the throne in every sense.
She will be an embellishment
to our dynasty, a sweet joy
in old age. O chase this sunlight
not from the snow of your white head!
This girl you will warm to, and she'll
enchant you as she enchants me.

KING.

Silence, you have no idea
what I think where it concerns you.
Listen here, my son, I can wear
the face of a bull and I would
rather not have you on my horns.
Step aside, here in the black, so
we can have a word in the dark,
quietly resolve our discord.

PRINCE.

Don't you want to see her?

KING.

I came with her in my mind's eye,
already caught up in this dream.
I feel quite well disposed towards her,
but don't take this to mean that now
I'm no longer opposed to you.
Step to the side here and you will
learn my fatherly intentions.

They step back into the gallery so that only their heads can be seen.

CINDERELLA (*upon awaking*).

Now I would love to know if I
can feel around with these hands.
If it's a dream, there is nothing.
For dreams, even if they please us,
they just aren't worth getting up for.
I want to move this foot—like so—
and now this hand, and now the head.
The gallery above, from which
that sweet man leant over to me,
is really and truly there, though
I don't remember and can't ask
how a prince came to bow to me.
Be what it will, the matter here
shan't fade away so quickly yet.
Maybe it never happened then.
I only just dreamt about it
in a dream while falling asleep.
But this head and that smile happened
as if in some reality
which was mine before sleep. Sleep has

made me mistrustful and timid.
It has ruined the game in which
I was so blissfully forlorn.
Now I'll take a few steps and see
if I can still walk. My eyes go
round in a circle and see
everything spic and span, indeed
not mysterious in the least,
as I would want it. Well, this has,
everything thus far said, has time.
The sisters come.

Both sisters enter.

FIRST SISTER.
Hey, Cinderella!

SECOND SISTER.
'Here,' she will say. 'I'll be right there'
is her lamely putting us off.

CINDERELLA.
Don't be angry for I'm here now.
On my knees if you so desire,
kissing you hand and foot. Never
have I been so quick and ready
to serve, so happy to obey.
Please tell me what I am to do.

SECOND SISTER.
Tie up the shoe on my foot here.

FIRST SISTER.
Go to the shoemaker for me.

CINDERELLA.

I will gladly jump for you soon,
but there's a tie that binds me here.
And when I'm so bound, my zeal flies
away for the sister who makes
me go. Then upon my return,
only weariness shall stand
in my place to serve you anew.
You will never see me weary
so long as you don't allow it.

SECOND SISTER.

This is really laced up too tight,
you lazy clod, here! Take that!

She pushes her away.

FIRST SISTER.

Leave, make off with you, and don't you
dawdle on the streets and corners.

CINDERELLA *exits.*

PRINCE (*in the gallery*).

Doesn't that vain pair of sisters
brood there like hate and resentment?
How slender they are—beautiful
if their natures were not ravaged
by ignorance, livid envy.
Yes, like sinister clouds, they blow
about this sweet, sunny image,
their little sister who is wholly
intimidated by their power

and no more knows to help herself.
This ought to be a fairy tale
for children—and grown-ups as well—
these two towers of fashion there
and the little deer they despise,
despise for being so beautiful.
Where would it flee? It's fit to make
the leap only too well, I think.
That it flee me I dread always.
Hey there, you sisters!

FIRST SISTER (*looking around*).
What does this big brute want?

SECOND SISTER.
Look you, you are too crude for us.
Go about your nasty business,
rouse your dogs, clutch your big skewer,
go shoot a rabbit to death. Here's
no place for such an ill-bred boy.

PRINCE.
Yes, indeed, all is good!

FIRST SISTER.
Leave the fool to himself, sister.

They speak to each other.
CINDERELLA *enters unnoticed.*

PRINCE (*softly*).
You nightingale, you lovely dream,
you, above every fantasy,
a sublime apparition, see

how quick my hands come together
in their veneration of you.
The language must be a weasel
falling headlong when it wishes
that it didn't lack words for her,
but it can see her poverty.
The wonder of her seals its lips.
In this way does love hold its breath.

CINDERELLA (*smiling*).

Be still—you harumpher—be still!*

PRINCE.

My father desires to see you
upon his lap as his crowned child.

CINDERELLA.

Is he an older man? Is he
the country's king?

PRINCE.

Yes, indeed he is. I'm his son.
Just now he called me a rascal
who leads him around by his big nose.
Now he's smiling and shedding tears
that stream down his big round full cheeks.
But when I asked him why he cried,
suddenly I'm a rapscallion,
a man ignorant of honour,
a thief of supreme majesty,
a perfect criminal. So I

* Possibly directed at the King, the audience or even the reader.

keep quiet, quiet as a mouse,
and I will not disturb his sleep
while he dreams of your elegance.

CINDERELLA.

And if that's what he's doing, won't he
be a rascal to you as well?

PRINCE.

Absolutely.

CINDERELLA.

Now hide yourself.

PRINCE *returns to his previous position.*

CINDERELLA.

Laugh quietly my angels who
hover in the air around me,
they point out at the heads up there,
the ones above this gallery,
which are somewhat half visible.
Just look at that gigantic crown
which deserves such a hearty laugh.
Look at that knotted knitted brow.
Now behold the head of a youth
and think hard about who it is.
The prince, assuredly, it is not.
His head perhaps, but it's not, too,
because surely a half a head
cannot be taken for the head.
The nice thing about this charade
is that you must laugh in silence,
very softly so no one hears,

especially my two sisters
who exist apart from laughter,
who would be taken aback and
yet don't feel it. Indeed, there is
someone sleeping in the great hall.
It's as if empathy were packed
in a matchbox. I'm tired as well
from putting all this into words.
This gallery column right here
will do as my little cradle.

She leans on a column.
FAIRY TALE, *fantastically garbed, appears from behind* PRINCE's *and* KING's *back.*

FAIRY TALE (*whispering*).
Cinderella!

CINDERELLA (*stepping forward*).
Well, now what's this? Who are you? Speak!

FAIRY TALE.
I am Fairy Tale, from whose lips
everything spoken here resounds,
from whose hand these images' charm,
which here enchant, take flight and go,
which can wake your feelings of love
with sweet gifts intended for you.
Observe, these dresses will make you
the most beautiful young lady,
place the hand of the Prince in yours.
Look at the way this one sparkles,
how this one flashes. Precious stones,

pearls, corals, which readily wish
to adorn your breast, to fetter
gracefully neck and arm. Take them,
and do take it, this dress and all.

She lets the dress fall to the ground.

If it should feel too tight on you,
don't worry, an elegant dress
presses itself tight to one's limbs,
eagerly fitting the body.
Now, let us move on to the shoes.
I believe that you have small feet,
very petite, the kind he likes.
Won't you be wanting shoes as well?

She holds them up high.

CINDERELLA.

You're blinding me.

FAIRY TALE.

I came here to leave you in awe.
People do not believe in me,
but so what when just my being near
makes them think a little again.
These shoes are silver but as light
as swan's down. I simply ask you
to hold them nimbly in your hands.

She throws them into CINDERELLA's *hands.*

CINDERELLA.

Oh!

FAIRY TALE.

Don't taunt your sisters with them.
Be noble with such noble splendour
while comporting yourself this way,
as your nature obligates you.

CINDERELLA.

O, I promise you.

FAIRY TALE.

You are a dear, sweet child worthy
of this fairy tale. Do not kneel!
I beg you, if I am dear to you,
kneel for her whom I kneel before.

CINDERELLA (*kneeling*).

No, let me. Gratefulness surely
feels itself divinely enriched.

FAIRY TALE.

It is due to your mother* that
I come to you. Such a woman
as lovely as her lives no more,
ornamented by such virtue
that virtue was made lovelier
than her, the loveliest—alive
no longer save, perhaps, in you.
You have what's sweetest about her,
something that makes women divine,
this alluring serenity

* In all the variations of the Cinderella story, her dead mother in some liminal or ghostly form ensures that her daughter is rewarded for her conduct.

which exists in a noble mind,
this inexpressible something
before which brave men kneel. Be still.
Put on that dress now in silence.
Slip into the palace tonight.
You know the rest of the story.
It's been dreamt long enough. This scene
must come to life now. To wonder
shall bring fear. And the fairy tale
goes on until its end, its home.

She exits.

CINDERELLA.

Now hurry, lest the sisters see me
too soon and I would come to grief
too late. A whim would have me
linger here, but a lucky girl
cannot marry a banterer,
she who must flee with her rich things,
hide them. A fancy would have me
smile here, and yet this happiness,
this smiling, is laughing me onwards.
Hurry, lest the Prince see me like this!

She exits.

PRINCE.

Hey, Cinderella!

KING.

Night has fallen, let's go home now.

PRINCE.

I must stay here for ever.

Three girls dressed as pages appear.

FIRST PAGE.

How funny I feel in these clothes.
They have made me look like a boy.

SECOND PAGE.

Mine tingles. It snags. It itches.
It's an unnameable feeling.
It kisses my entire body.

FIRST PAGE.

As I pulled them on over me,
a fire blasted me in the face.
I wear them now, but I don't know
how I shall ever keep them on.

THIRD PAGE.

I feel like doing what boys will do.
I want to jump, to laugh, to twirl
my arms and my legs to and fro
and yet I can't. Like a sin they
are squeezing my fair young body,
making me grow stiff.

FIRST PAGE.

But not even for a kingdom
would I not love to feel such fear.
To me they hurt so well and so
pleasurably at the same time.

SECOND PAGE.

When the heavens and the earth lay
one atop the other, they'd feel
half so tightly pressed together
compared to this attire and me.

FIRST PAGE.

Girls, the Prince calls.

PRINCE.

What do you want? Why are you here?

FIRST PAGE.

To grace the scene the way your dream
and the fairy tale desire it.
For decoration, we have draped
the gallery in precious cloth.
Now we'll puff perfume everywhere
to fill the room with its scent.
Now we'll light the candelabra
and make the night as bright as day.
If you still have orders,
tell us.

SECOND PAGE.

Shall we assemble the people
to applaud this celebration?

PRINCE.

No, no, not that kind of celebration,
not what you think, which needs people,
which is enframed with their cheers.
We'll have a celebration with ourselves,
a totally silent one,
where the public voice gets nothing
to trumpet and the world nothing
to concern itself. Heedlessness
celebrates here, a festive mood
filling our hearts, without worry.

Nor would we make much of a crowd
for any bothersome fellow,
since we would have no need of pomp
or vain splendour, which here never
has to see to our happiness.
I feel such silent happiness,
such a sweet and holy feeling,
that to think about a party
feels reprehensible to me.
I already felt festive here,
even before you brought candles
to light the feast. An anxious joy,
who's half ashamed and half happy,
who's an untold bundle of nerves,
who doubts in her success, she is
the party-giver here.

THIRD PAGE.

Just this slender column's to do,
my lord, spinning me like a bride.

PRINCE.

Now do me this favour and leave.
Accept my gratitude for your work.

FIRST PAGE.

Those here are finely bred pages,
leaving when there is no more need.

SECOND PAGE.

Come away. This page to a prince
is but a dream.

The PAGES *exit.*

PRINCE.

I conduct myself in a dream
so much now, I could easily
submit to a foreign power.
Is what I see before my eyes
my possession? Am I indeed
not set up as though in a game?
Haven't I sat here long enough,
while nothing will move me forward?
I really think I am going mad
and all this, what is around me,
seems no less by the agency
of magic. However, as said,
I want domination, shackles.
My blood, although it is princely,
feels very well under such bonds,
more than well. I would love to shout,
I'd love to shout with such a voice
that the echo would fade away
above the whole world. O how nice
bondage is here that otherwise
darkens the place in which it reigns.
I have never felt so anxious
for the miraculous image
that comes when the story's over.
The end of this thing here must be
a miracle, for it makes me
suffer to wait so. Hey, Father!

KING.

This is getting painful. Come home.

PRINCE.

My home will be forever here.
I feel every single moment
like a kiss. The passage of time
touches my cheeks caressingly,
my senses draw towards this perfume.
I will cling to this world here
as she to me. I will not come
away, not ever.

KING.

And what if I order you now?

PRINCE.

You've neither say nor power here.
I give myself the final word.
I confer power on myself
which says not to listen to you.
Forgive me, Father, in me is
a rebellious, youthful impulse,
one you had too when you were young.
I'll stay and wait here till life stirs.

KING.

Well must I too. But this hand has
yet to be extended, has yet
to forgive you for your speech.

PRINCE.

It is so infinitely dear
to forgive, so sweet to the one
who does so over and over.
That you'd surely forgive me
I knew for certain.

KING.

Such pish-posh!

PRINCE.

I will forget that this strikes me
as rather strange, such that even
anticipation keeps silent
and her conduct remains concealed
by a question. Yes, I am here
in a place so well beloved
that I can perhaps be patient.
But I am bothered by one thought:
Just where is Cinderella now?
Eh? What if she doesn't come back?
What if she utterly forgets
just where her empathies belong?
This is improbable but not
unlikely. That which is likely
is a wide world, and that a thing
happened was already likely,
even while seeming unlikely,
is almost beyond my grasp too.
And what is likely beyond me
is still as good as being likely.
So be it. I will get a hold
of myself. It befits someone,
especially men, to be proud.
But what is the fear in pride then,
what affects it so? And such pride,
what could it be worth to yourself?
No, I wish to weep, that this child
far from me so long has a chance.

I want to think that only this
will ever be.

KING.

I fear, as I stand here loafing,
my country totters. Let it fall
into chaos. The fairy tale
draws to an end and tickles
my fancy. Afterwards will I
be the divine order once more.
Government enjoys its sleep too,
and the father of the law is
only human.

PRINCE.

I would willingly hold my breath
to hear her step all the better.
Yet she has such a light footstep
that even this inkling can't tell
when she approaches. O she draws
near, here to this impatient sense,
whose muscles tear themselves apart
to feel her near. The way being near
can be so sweet when it involves
the lover, and how gruff she is
when a thing bad oppresses us.
Here only the delightful should
really be what oppresses us,
and yet this is never love's way.
She's silent where she must forget,
she doesn't have this loud echo

which signals falsehood. O she is
rich, and words aren't necessary
to remember her by. Surely,
O surely this dearest creature
cannot be far. My feeling says
this with spirit. Just the patience
to not evade who bides her time
is the one thing I think about.
I must stand here, standing as firm
as if some word could order me.
Lovers happily wait. To dream
of the beloved makes time fly.
What is time but just a quarrel
of impatience now becalmed?
What's that shining there upon me?

He comes down from the gallery.

KING.

I don't understand this matter,
why I'm married to silence here.
I'm too old for marriage. Reason
scolds me, points a finger at me,
it laughs out loud, but what is wrong?
I'm old, of course, and have a right
to be foolish. This indulgence
merrily takes the common path
with white hair. I indulge my son,
that he boldly play my warden.
Out of caprice, which as you know
skips behind at my age, I'll drop it,

as the spirit of youth would want.
I'm falling asleep—fatigue sits
well in my silver hair, like sleep
to my ancient, head-shaking brain.

PRINCE (*below, with a shoe in his hand*).
I see this thing as a portent
to approaching glory and love.
It's a slipper for a fine foot.
It speaks of a pleasing nature
as if it had a mouth, a gift
for eloquence. And these fine jewels
do not belong to her sisters,
who have turned to stone over there.
Where would they get such a foot too,
so narrowly shaped for this shoe?
Just whom could it belong to then?
I don't want to face this question.
It scares me. Could it really be?
Does it belong to that girl? No,
I torture myself needlessly.
Who would give her silver and gold,
who would give her such royal jewels?
And yet some feeling speaks to me
of Cinderella, which reveals
her strange behaviour, her distance,
her style. Magic, as I well know,
is a possibility here.
I want to want it, for I can't
hold it, cannot get a grasp.

He climbs up the staircase reflectively, stalking CINDERELLA *above in a maid's dress, carrying* FAIRY TALE*'s gifts in her arms.*

CINDERELLA.

How is it you're still here, my Prince?

PRINCE.

I am still here, my charming child,
only to behold you once more.
What have you there?

CINDERELLA.

See, they are beautiful clothes! Look
greedily at this finery.
Such would bring joy to a king's eye.

PRINCE.

Who gave you that?

CINDERELLA.

O that wouldn't interest you much.
I don't even know exactly.
It's enough these sweet things are mine
and that I can put them on now
if I wanted to. But—

PRINCE.

But—

CINDERELLA.

I no more do.

PRINCE.

What has made you so strangely cold?
Who clouded the lake of your soul
with silt, such that it looks so dark?

CINDERELLA.

I myself, and so just be still,
please put aside your noble wrath.
There will be no more hurting here.
Only—

PRINCE.

What? Tell me, love!

CINDERELLA.

Only that something still pains me:
among all these lovely things here,
something is still missing. I must be
missing my left slipper—aha,
that's it, of course.

PRINCE.

Well, of course—and is this one yours?

CINDERELLA.

How can you ask? It is just like
its brother here on the table.
So then I have this splendid gift
in full, and so I can go forth.

PRINCE.

Aren't you going to wear these around
your body, your lovely body?

CINDERELLA.

Not these!

PRINCE.

What's gotten into you suddenly?

CINDERELLA.

So suddenly—what is it then?

PRINCE.

That you don't love me any more?

CINDERELLA.

I don't know whether I love you.
Yet again it's clear I love you,
for what kind of girl would not love
the high station and manliness,
the nobility, the fine cast?
I love your majesty, which is
so patient and awaits my own.
I am touched that you, you alone
have shown such compassion for me.
Something touches me to the quick.
I'm nervous all of a sudden.
I stand utterly, miserably
exposed here. The least little breeze
will blow my heart into a storm,
to be so still soon afterwards,
the same way it lies outspread now,
just like a peaceful, sunlit lake.

PRINCE.

Does your heart really feel like this?

CINDERELLA.

Like this and different. What one word
might express. Our language sounds
far too crude for expressing this.
Music is required to better

say this over and over. It,
it is playing.

Music.

PRINCE.

Listen, what lovely dance music.
Desire rises, swells inside me,
and I can no longer bear it,
that we stand here ever longer,
dithering. Come, let me lead you
in dance. Our ball begins here now,
with our own magic power. Drop
that silver-heavy burden, come.

CINDERELLA.

In this dress, my lord, full of filth
and covered with stains? So you want
to dance with a kitchen apron,
hold on tight to its soot and dust?
I would be thinking otherwise,
before I did such a thing.

PRINCE.

Not me.

He carries her down the steps.
When he is below:

A princely pair dances.

They dance. After a few rounds, the music stops.

CINDERELLA.

Look, look!

PRINCE.

Like it's warning us to be still.

CINDERELLA.

It wants this too. It's a very
sensitive creature, not wanting
its sound to be lost in the dance.
It shows our imagination
is alive: we dance in a dream
as well as if it were real. In this case
a dance does not want to be danced,
crashed about. Empathy can dance,
with no foot, with no sound as well.
Quiet, for we must listen, it's
what this music wants from us too!

The music begins anew.

PRINCE.

Listen, as sweet as any dream.

CINDERELLA.

Yes, it is a dream, so subtly
does it stir the dream inside us.
O how it can't bear a vast space.
It escapes into the silence,
where it moves nothing but the air
slowly back and forth. Let us sink
completely into its substance.
Thereafter we will forget what
we must forget. Let us seek out
the trail that leads to empathy,
the one we lost in our vulgar

passions. It will not be easy
to find this sweetness. It requires
infinite patience, like a sense
rarely achieved. It's so easy,
like when we wish to comprehend
the incomprehensible. Come,
let's rest in bliss.

PRINCE.

Your words ring as sweet as music.

CINDERELLA.

Hush, don't disturb me in this thought,
which, half released, gives me such pain.
Once it gets out, I'll be happy
and cheerful, as you would want me.
But it will never leave its cell,
this sense of being forsaken, which
I feel rising up in my heart.
It will fade away like a sound,
faint, guilty; and the memory
will never die. A part remains
with me until, perchance, there comes
some freak thing to save me from it.

PRINCE.

So what is this thought of yours then?

CINDERELLA.

Nothing, nothing at all—a whim.
When we hang on to a scruple
for much too long—something stupid—
yet which provides us with no end,
since a beginning, middle, end
are all but shifting things, never

with any sense, never, ever
knowing one's heart. The end is:
I will be happy with you now.

PRINCE.

How you move me, and how you charm
me with your impulsivity,
which, with every indication,
has this noble bearing. We will
forget who and just what we are,
share happiness, like the anguish
we sincerely shared. You're quiet?

CINDERELLA.

Rather the captured nightingale,
one who sits trembling in its snare,
forgetting the song she would sing.

PRINCE.

You so please me!

CINDERELLA.

I'm all yours, so frightfully yours
that you must lend me your body
to hide myself deep inside it.

PRINCE.

I shall offer you a kingdom—

CINDERELLA.

No, no!

PRINCE.

—a villa, in which you will dwell.
It is tucked deep in a garden.
Your view will come to rest on trees,
on flowers, the dense greenery,

on ivy garlanding the wall,
on a sky that sends you sunlight
more gorgeous than any other
as it pierces chinks in the leaves.
Moonlight there is more sensitive,
the tips of the pine trees tickle
it raw and tender. The birdsong
is to your ears a recital
inexpressibly beautiful.
As its mistress, you will wander
through the design of this garden,
upon paths that, as though they could
have feelings, part ways and rejoin
suddenly. Fountains brighten you,
the dreamer, whenever you dwell
in your thoughts too much. All of this
will come running to wait on you
and simply when it pleases you,
all feeling according to you,
all cheerfully subservient.

CINDERELLA.

You banter with me. Isn't it,
isn't it true that I would feel
myself borne by hands? By your hand,
there is no doubt I'd be clinging
utterly and blissfully so.
But these clothes* here, you see, those that
I am miserably attached to.

* The gifts from Fairy Tale as well as Cinderella's kitchen clothes can be read into this speech.

I would have to put them aside,
no more to be Cinderella—

PRINCE.

Then you will have handmaidens and
wardrobes full of gorgeous dresses.

CINDERELLA.

So, will I then?

PRINCE.

All day long in silence you would
be left to yourself. Only when
desire drove you from the garden
to people and to greater noise,
as it met your stillness, would you
find in the palace murmuring
enough delight, glitter, splendour,
music, dance, frolic, what you will.

CINDERELLA.

This again would make for something
like a very pleasant and lovely
contrast to my solitude then.
Do you think so?

PRINCE.

Of course.

CINDERELLA.

How I love you. I cannot find,
in that wide, open, infinite
land of gratitude, one small word
to thank you. So let me, in place
of every way to express thanks,

kiss you, like this. O that was sweet.
Good, now that it is at an end.

PRINCE.

An end? To what?

CINDERELLA.

This leaping comes to an end now,
this dance with me. I'm not for you.
I'm still but promised to myself.
Memory reminds me I've not
yet dreamt this love through to the end,
that something floats around me here,
something here, something that gives me
still much more to do. Don't you see
the quiet sisters over there,
hard as stone, watching us amazed?
I feel sorry for them, although
they're not worth feeling sorry for.
But that is not being true, it is
only said for my sake really.
I love them, who worked me so hard
and stern. I love the punishment
which was undeserved, the foul words,
so as to keep smiling brightly.
I get endless satisfaction.
It occupies me all day long,
gives me cause to leap and to see,
to think and to dream. And that is
the reason I am such a dreamer.
I was betrothed to you too soon.

You deserve someone better.
The fairy tale never tells this.

PRINCE.

The fairy tale wants it. It's clear,
the fairy tale will see us wed.

CINDERELLA.

A wide-awake fairy tale is
inside this dreaming creature here.
And I couldn't dream at your side!

PRINCE.

But, but—!

CINDERELLA.

No, not where I would be displayed
like I was a bird in a cage.
I couldn't take that, not being able
to kiss.

PRINCE.

But if you want to see it fly,
should you not expend some effort
to chase after it? You only dream
when you have to catch a dream.

CINDERELLA.

How nice you understand me. True,
so true.

PRINCE.

Now, now, compose yourself. I know
you're now going to put this dress on,
which the Fairy Tale chose for you.

You were born to have such sweet things
and you can't escape these fetters,
ten thousand many caprices
which all rise up inside of you.
May I conduct you towards the door?

They stand up.

See, it would be a shame for you.
This fineness you have inside you
ordains that you will be my wife.
You cry?

CINDERELLA.

For I must follow you despite
the aforesaid and so gladly
will I follow you from now on.

PRINCE.

I ask very, very much.

CINDERELLA *gathers up the dresses and exits.*

Hey, Father!

KING (*from above*).

What kind of a girl is that, son?

PRINCE.

Is she good enough now?

KING.

As a goddess she shall ascend
to my throne. Her ennoblement
shall stir the land into music
and revelry. I'll be right down
and proclaim it to our nation.

In the meantime she'll come with you
amid rejoicing, which like incense
will lead, follow.

He exits.

PRINCE.
I'll wait here until her return.

To CINDERELLA, *who appears above in the gallery in her extravagant dress.*

Ah, is it you?

CINDERELLA.
To serve you, lord.

PRINCE.
O dear, no! O how — — —

He leaps up the stairs towards her.

CINDERELLA.
Yes, yes.

SNOW WHITE

(1901)

A garden. To the right, the palace entrance.
In the background, rolling mountains.
QUEEN, SNOW WHITE, *the foreign* PRINCE, HUNTER.

QUEEN.

Say, are you sick?

SNOW WHITE.

You would ask since you wanted death
on the one who always stung you
in the eyes as too beautiful.
How you look at me so composed.
This kindness, showing in your eyes,
so full of love, is just made up,
the serene tone just counterfeit.
Hate really does dwell in your heart.
You dispatched the Hunter to me
and told him to draw his dagger,
to point it at this despised face.
You ask me whether I'm sick now?
Such sport sounds bad from a soft voice.

Indeed, softness becomes sly sport
when it is so fearlessly cruel.
I'm not sick—I'm very much dead.
The poison apple was painful,
O, O so painful, and Mother, you,
you're the one who brought it to me.
So why joke about my being sick?

QUEEN.

Fair child, you are wrong. You are sick,
no, gravely, very gravely ill.
There's no doubt this fresh garden air
will do you good. I beg of you,
just don't let your weak little head
give in to the idea. Be still.
Don't mull things over and over.
Get some exercise, skip and run.
Shout while chasing a butterfly.
Scold the air for not making it
warm enough yet. Become a child.
Soon you'll leave this colour behind,
which is like a pale winding sheet
draped over your pink complexion.
Think not of sin. The sin should be
forgotten. Perhaps I did sin
against you many long years ago.
Who could remember such a thing?
Unpleasant things are easily
forgotten if you consider
who's near and dear. Are you crying?

SNOW WHITE.

Yes, I must when I realize
how quick you are to wring the past
by the neck the way you wanted
mine wrung. Crying, of course, over
the sinful absent mind which wants
to sweet-talk me. O how you give
this sin such wings, and yet it flies
terribly with this new pair
which doesn't fit. It lies so close
to me and you, this thing you want
bantered away with a sweet word,
so close, I'd say, close to the touch,
such that I can never forget it,
nor you who committed it.
Hunter, speak, you did swear my death?

HUNTER.

Of course, Princess, a grisly death,
just not performed as loud and clear
as the fairy tale heralded.
The humble way you begged touched me,
your face, lying there sweet as snow
beneath the kiss of the sunlight.
I sheathed that which I intended
for your murder, stabbing the deer
which leapt across our path. I sucked
the blood out of it greedily.
Yours, however, I left untouched.
So don't say I swore you should die.
I took pity and broke my oath
before I did you any harm.

QUEEN.

So what are you crying about?
He drew his dagger for the fun.
He'd have to stab what's soft in him
before he could ever stab you.
But he didn't. The soft in him
is alive like the morning sun.
Come give me a kiss and forget.
Look up with joy and show some sense.

SNOW WHITE.

How can I kiss the lips of one
who pushed this Hunter off, kissed him
into doing the bloody deed.
I'll never kiss you. With kisses
you fired the Hunter to murder
and my death was seconds away,
because he was your sweet lover.

QUEEN.

What did you say?

HUNTER.

Me with kisses?

PRINCE.

I really believe it's all true.
That man in the green jacket has
far less respect than befits him
in the presence of this great Queen.
Snow White, O how evilly have
you been played by such ruthless hate.
It's a wonder that you're alive.

You survived poison and a knife.
From what stuff are you made,
for you're dead and yet so lovely
alive, indeed, so little dead
that life must be in love with you?
Tell me, did the Hunter stab you?

SNOW WHITE.

No, no, there beats in this fellow
a good heart filled with compassion.
If the Queen had this heart, she would
be a better mother to me.

QUEEN.

I mean to be much better with you
than your keen suspicion suggests.
I did not send the Hunter off
after you with kisses. Blind fear
has made you too apprehensive.
In fact, I have always loved you
as my sweet, innocent child.
Why would I have any reason,
cause, or right to hate one as dear
to me as a child of my own breast!
O do not believe that coy voice
whispering of sin, which it's not.
Believe your right, not your left ear,
I mean that false one telling you
that I am this evil mother
green-eyed at beauty. Don't be fooled
by such an absurd fairy tale

stuffing the world's greedy ears full
of these newsy bits that I am
mad with jealousy, by nature
evil. It is just idle talk.
I love you. To admit this has
never been said more sincerely.
That you're so lovely gives me joy.
Beauty in one's own child is balm
for a mother's love gone weary,
not the goad to some heinous deed,
like the fairy tale has laid out
for this storyline here, this play.
Don't turn away. Be a dear child.
Trust a parent's word as your own.

SNOW WHITE.

O I believed you with pleasure,
for believing is quiet bliss.
But how much faith is going to make
me believe when no faith exists,
where a roguish malice lurks, where
injustice sits with a proud neck?
You speak as kindly as you can,
and yet you still cannot act kind.
Those eyes, flashing so scornfully,
scowl at me so threatening, so
unmotherly, laugh with menace
at the affection on your tongue,
with derision. They speak the truth,
those proud eyes and they alone I
believe, not the betrayer's tongue.

PRINCE.

I believe you see right, my child.

QUEEN.

Must you keep helping, little Prince,*
feeding more flames to the fire where
a flood of healing is needed?
A stranger clad in motley clothes
should not step too close to a queen.

PRINCE.

Why not dare to rise against you,
you fiend, for the Princess' sake?

QUEEN.

What?

PRINCE.

Yes, and while I look small and weak,
I'll echo this a thousand times,
ten—a hundred thousand times for you:
a dreadful crime's taken place here,
and one that points to you, the Queen.
Poison was strewn for this sweet child,
set out as though she were a dog.
Why not admit your wickedness,
your good conscience! You, fair child,
let's go upstairs now for a bit
and contemplate this grievous thing.
If you're too weak, just lay your head
upon my faithful shoulder here,

*The Prince should be seen as shorter than the other characters, even Snow White, and wearing a chequered costume.

which would cherish such a burden.
From you, Queen, we shall take our leave
for now of a short span of time.
Then we'll continue our talk.
(*To* SNOW WHITE) Come,
permit me this sweet liberty.

He leads her inside the palace.

QUEEN.

Just go, broken mast and rigging.
Go newlyweds, married to death.
Go misery, lead weakness away,
and be very dear arm in arm.
Come, handsome Hunter, let us talk.

Change of scene.
A room inside the palace. PRINCE *and* SNOW WHITE.

PRINCE.

I would talk away the whole day
with you and do so arm in arm.
How strange this language is to me
which comes from that sweet mouth of yours.
Your mere word, how alive it is.
My ear hangs rapt on its richness
in a hammock of harkening
while dreaming of a violin strain,
a lisp, a fair nightingale's song,
of love's twittering. In and out
the dreaming goes like ocean waves
washing onto our garden shore.
O speak, and I'm ever asleep,

a prisoner of love this way,
in chains, yet infinitely rich,
free as no free man ever was.

SNOW WHITE.

You speak such noble princely speech.

PRINCE.

No, let me listen instead,
such that the love I swore below
in the garden, in that playpen,
never blows away in vain words.
I only want to listen and respond
to your love which rings in my head.
Speak, that I am ever silent
and true to you. Unfaithfulness
comes quick with words. It speaks rashly,
a fountain in the wind, being whipped,
to boil over into babble.
No, let me be silent, true to you.
In this sense, I shall love you more
than with love. Then wholeheartedness
knows itself no more. It showers
me in this wetness same as you.
Love is wet the way the night is,
such that dry dust never clouds it.
So speak, such that when you speak
it falls like dew upon our love.
You're quiet. What do you see there?

SNOW WHITE.

You do talk like a waterfall
of silence, yet you're not silent.

PRINCE.

What's wrong, speak! You look so sombre,
so plaintive right down to your toes,
as if you were searching for words
which whisper love. Do not sulk there.
Speak up when something troubles you.
Unroll it just like a carpet
on which we will merrily play.
To dally on one's heartache is good.

SNOW WHITE.

You talk for ever and promise
silence though. What are you saying,
talking headlong on and on?
Confidence is not so quick-tongued.
Love fancies it soft and serene.
O if you're not devoted
to my bliss in every sense,
then say so. Say it, for you say
unfaithfulness would talk away
eagerly, talkative, so fast.

PRINCE.

Let's let that go.

SNOW WHITE.

Yes, let's make small talk, be merry.
Let us banish from love's kingdom
melancholy and dolefulness.
Let's jest and dance and cheer aloud.
Why worry of the pain of now
which commands us to be silent!
Well, what see you in the garden?

PRINCE (*looking out the window*).

Alas, what I see is fair and sweet
to the naked eye which but sees.
To feeling, which takes in this scene
with its fine net, it is sacred.
To intellect, which knows the past,
it's disgusting, a dirty flood
of filthy water. O, it takes
a twofold view, sweet and terrible,
thoughtful and beautiful. Look there,
with your own eyes, see for yourself.

SNOW WHITE.

No, tell me what you see? Tell me.
From your lips, then I could gather
such a picture's subtle detail.
If you paint it, surely you will
cleverly, prudently temper
the view's poignancy. Now, what goes?
Rather than look, I'd rather hear.

PRINCE.

It is the most lovely passion
ever to inflame two lovers.
The Queen kisses the Hunter's lips,
and he gives kiss after kiss back.
They sit beneath the willow tree,
whose long branches flutter downwards
upon their heads. The grass kisses
the tangle of interlocked feet.
The wood bench sighs under the press
of their bodies making one body

in the rapture of their embrace.
O, so a tiger pair would mate
in the jungle, far from the real world.
The sweet bliss makes them one, tears them
apart just to bring them closer
all over again. I'm speechless,
without image at such image.
Will you see it and be speechless?

SNOW WHITE.

No, such a thing would disgust me.
Come away from that dirty scene.

PRINCE.

The colours barely release me
from its spell. It is a painting,
and sweet love is its painter.
O, how she lies down there, this Queen,
being crushed inside his strong arms.
How she cries from passion and how
her beau smothers her with kisses,
like one smothering a bowl of food,
no, a sky, this mouth opening
on heavenly passion itself.
That rogue is utterly shameless.
He thinks his green hunting jacket
protects him from barbs. Here's a barb,
what seems to bewitch me up here.
O, I'm driven mad. This lady!
Not this churl. O just the lady!
What damage the ruffian does.
Alas, this sweet, this sweet lady.—

If I could but shed the meaning
of what I've seen. Now I am lost.
A storm rages over it all,
what is called love, would still be called,
but no more. Away, everything.

SNOW WHITE.

Woe unto me that I must hear.

PRINCE.

Woe unto us that I must see.

SNOW WHITE.

O, how I long for nothing more
than to be smiling and dead, dead.
This I am too and always was.—
I've never felt life's seething storm.
I am as still as this soft snow,
which lies for a ray of sunlight,
that it takes it. Thus am I snow
and melt away with a warm breeze
meant not for me but for the spring.
Sweet is this seeping down. Dear earth,
receive me unto your dwelling!
The sun is too painful for me.

PRINCE.

Do I give you this terrible pain?

SNOW WHITE.

O no, not you. You could never!

PRINCE.

How lovely you are, how you laugh
for me, come smiling! Don't love me.

I simply disturb your repose.
O, to have left your coffin alone!
How beautiful you lay therein,
snow in a silent wintry world.

SNOW WHITE.

Snow, always snow?

PRINCE.

Forgive me, you dear winter scene,
you likeness of serene white calm.
If I upset you, it happened
only for love. Now this love turns
away from you again, weeping,
towards the Queen. Please forgive this love
for lifting you from that coffin,
the glass one, wherein you lay
with rosy cheeks, an open mouth,
and this breath just like one alive,
this picture to die for most sweet.
I should have left it just like that,
with love kneeling before you then.

SNOW WHITE.

Look, look! Now that I am alive
you dump me like a dead body!
How very strange you men all are.

PRINCE.

Rightly scold me, then you show love.
Hate me and I'll kneel before you.
If you called me a rotten knave
it would fit well. But let me now

find that lovely Queen, for I wish
to free her from a love unworthy.
I beg you be very angry
with me, indeed, be very mad.

SNOW WHITE.

Why then? Give me a reason why?

PRINCE.

Well, because I'm such a villain
to run from you to another,
she who excites his mind more now.

SNOW WHITE.

You are not a villain! Well, well—
that mind, that mind of yours is more
excited? What's on your mind is so
mindless. What a pack of dogs must
excite your mind such that you flee
like a terrified deer, the foe
pursuing you. Well, so be it.
So fly from me then to this stream
with the better water to lap.
I'll remain, smiling, teasing you
with my pale white hand outstretched,
follow your flight with a gay voice
that calls: Snow White shall wait for you.
Come, knock on this familiar door
and laugh aloud. And then you turn
your dear, faithful head to me
begging me to just be quiet,
for shouting serves no purpose.—Go!

O go then, for I release you.
And do commend me to my Queen.

PRINCE.

Commend you to the Queen? What for?
Am I dreaming?

SNOW WHITE.

Well, am I not allowed to send
my regards to Mummy with you,
who's down there in that shady park
occupied with her needlework?
She sews a token of her love—
what do I care. I owe her love,
and love sends its regards with you.
Say, I forgive her. No, not that.
Anyway, it doesn't show well
for a child to be on her knees
and begging for me to forgive.
You'll be half love's own already
on your knees. Then say it like so,
in passing, like sugared pastry,
and pay heed when she nods so fair,
when she's choking with emotion
and gives her hand for your hot kiss,
which sends, you being so chivalrous,
my forgiveness for this mistake.
How impatient I am for word
from my mother. So be quick, go!

PRINCE.

Snow White, I don't understand you.

SNOW WHITE.

That has nothing to do with it.
Go now, I beg of you. Leave this
flower to herself that can only
bloom in full in her solitude.
For she was never meant for you.
So calm down then. Depart, leave me
to dream here, to close myself up
as though some gaily coloured plant.
Go to this other flower, go,
draw upon her sweeter fragrance.

PRINCE.

You should calm down. Just wait here.
I shall bring the Queen back to you
reconciled. I'll look for her now
down there in her shady garden
and talk to that villain Hunter.
No matter where and when and how,
I'll find him too. So until then,
just remain calm and wait for us.

Exits.

SNOW WHITE.

He's filled with turmoil and counsels
calm in me that in richer measure
than his has possession of me.
Everything goes the way it must.
This untrue Prince has done me wrong.
But I'll not cry, the same way
I would not rejoice had I proof

of his innermost love for me.
Fury more than fury musters
I cannot do, and who silently
keeps silent chokes down fear, so
this I will do. O my, here comes
Mother herself and all alone.

To QUEEN, *who enters.*

O kind Mother, O forgive me.

She throws herself at her feet.

QUEEN.
What is this for, my child? Get up.

SNOW WHITE.
No, I kneel like this for your sake.

QUEEN.
What's with you, what makes you this way,
what quivers like this in your breast?
Stand up and tell me what is wrong.

SNOW WHITE.
Do not withdraw this gentle hand,
which I would cover with kisses.
How much have I longed for its clasp!
A shyer plea for forgiveness
has never been made as shyly
as mine to you. Forget, forgive.
Please be my merciful mother.
Let me be your good little girl
who frightened clasps to your body.
O sweet hand, I had thought of you,

you coming for my life, offering
me the apple—something not true.
Sin so fine is only contrived
of recalling all kinds of things.
My thinking is the only sin
there is here. O please absolve me
of that suspicion which wronged you.
I only want to love, love you.

QUEEN.

What? Did I not send the Hunter?
Did I not spur him on with kisses
to you to do this great, great sin?
You know that you're not thinking right.

SNOW WHITE.

I just feel! A feeling thinks sharp.
It knows every little detail
of this matter. A feeling,
far more noble than to recall,
will think a situation through,
but to forgive. And its judgement,
which is devoid of all judgement,
judges more severe, simply too.
So I see nothing in thinking.
It just speculates here and there,
full of big airs and opinions,
says this happened like so and keeps
making petty condemnations.
Away with the judge who but thinks!
If he can't feel, he must think small.

His verdict gives one stomach pains.
It's weak and drives accusers mad.
It absolves the sinner of sin,
dropping the charges in one breath.
Go and fetch me this other judge,
this sweet, ignorant feeling. Hear
what it says. Oh, it says nothing.
It smiles, kisses the sin to death,
caresses it like its sister,
chokes her with kisses. My feeling
absolves you of all sin. It lies
before you on beseeching knees
and begs, calls me sinner, me who
pleads so frightened for forgiveness.

QUEEN.

The poison apple I sent you—
you took a bite, of course, and died.
The dwarfs bore you in the coffin,
the one of glass, until the kiss
of the Prince brought you back to life.
That is what happened, am I right?

SNOW WHITE.

All of it's true up to the kiss.
The defiling mouth of a man
has never before kissed these lips.
The Prince, and how he could kiss too—
he had no hair upon his chin.
He's still a little boy, elsewise
noble, but so very short, weak,

like the body in which he's trapped,
small, like the mind he depends on.
Of one Prince's kiss say nothing more
of it, Mummy. The kiss is dead,
for he never sensed the wetness
on both sides of two moistened lips.
What did I want to talk about?
Ah, of sin, that stands on its knees,
before you, of the dear sinner.

QUEEN.

No, that is wrong. You yourself tell
such fairy-tale lies. Surely it
says that I am an evil queen,
that I dispatched the Hunter to you,
and gave you the apple to eat.
Now answer me straight about this.
Your begging me for forgiveness
is just a joke, isn't that true?
All of this gesture and technique
is rehearsed, a script cleverly
practised by you yourself. You have,
as it turns out, only made me
suspicious. What are you doing now?

SNOW WHITE.

Looking upon your kind, soft hand,
seeing its beauty wondrously
waking in a child a feeling
almost totally extinguished.
No, you are no sinner at all:

where would you get this idea?
Neither am I. We're still spotless
of all guilt, immaculately
watching an immaculate sky
being as mild as it has been here.
Once we did evil to ourselves.
But that is far too long ago
to remember. Now part for me,
I beg you, those dear lips of yours.
Tell me what will make me happy.

QUEEN.

I sent you off to die sparing
not one kiss or caress on him,
who followed you like a wild beast,
hunting you through woods and fields
until you fell down to the ground.

SNOW WHITE.

Ah, yes, I know the story well,
about the apple, the coffin.
Be so kind as to tell me more.
Why does nothing else come to mind?
Must you hang on to these details?
Must you forever draw on them?

QUEEN.

With kisses, kisses I fired on
the Hunter, my bloodthirsty man.
O, how the kisses came raining
like drops of dew upon that face
swearing faith to me, harm to you.

SNOW WHITE.

Forget about it, my dear Queen.
I beg you think no more of it.
Do not roll your big eyes like that.
Why do you shake? You've only
been good to me all of your life,
for which I'm utterly grateful.
If love knew of a better word,
then it might speak less awkwardly.
Love is boundless for that reason.
It knows to say nothing when it's
wholly enrapt in your being.
Hate me so that I can but love
more childlike, more intimately
and lovingly in solitude,
for no other reason than that
love is sweet and ambrosial
to one who humbly offers it.
Don't you hate me?

QUEEN.

I hate myself much more than you.
Once I did hate you, begrudging
your beauty despite the whole world,
for the whole world sang your praises,
gave you homage while I, the Queen,
was looked upon suspiciously.
O did that make my blood boil.
It turned me into this tigress.
I didn't see with my own eyes.
I didn't hear with my own ears.

Unfounded hate but saw and heard,
ate, dreamt, performed and slept for me.
I lay sadly ear to pillow,
did what hate did. That's in the past.
Hate now wants to love. And love hates
itself for not loving harder.
Why look, there comes the young Prince.
Go, kiss him, call him your precious.
Tell him I shall be nice to him
despite his bitter words spoken
in your favour. Go and tell him!

PRINCE *enters.*

PRINCE.
Fair Queen, I've been looking for you.

QUEEN.
Fair? Such a chivalrous greeting.
I do like you, Prince, Snow White's half,
to whom you wish to be married.

PRINCE.
Snow White wants not to be my bride.
She says I've had a change of heart
since lifting her from the coffin
and leading her here. And she's right,
so you're to blame, and to you, Queen,
I utterly devote myself.

QUEEN.
Where is this weak temperament,
which like a reed shakes back and forth
when the wind blows, going to take us?

PRINCE.

Where? I don't really know where.
But this I know only too well,
that I am in love, and with whom?
With you, with the Queen that you are.

QUEEN.

Such love, ah, that doesn't suit me.
This is too fast. Your behaviour
I find perfectly juvenile.
Your mind is far too capricious,
your nature too rash. Have patience
and don't tell me that you love me.
In fact, you need to be scolding me
still, Snow White's half, she whom you seem
to rather carelessly forget.
Hey, Hunter.

PRINCE.

What of that villain?

QUEEN.

He's no villain. In hunter's clothes,
he equals ten thousand princes.
Don't be a hothead. Think of who's
present when you stir up your storm.

To HUNTER, *who appears.*

Oh, there you are.

HUNTER.

What's your bidding?

QUEEN.

As though it were real, re-enact
that scene of Snow White's distress,
of what happened in the forest.
Do it like you wanted her dead.
You, girl, beg as though you mean it.
The Prince and I, we will only watch
and critique if you play your roles
too lightly. Now then, let's begin!

HUNTER.

Snow White, come, I'm going to kill you.

SNOW WHITE.

Oh, like it happened that quickly.
First draw your dagger. I'm not scared
at all of your proud booming voice.
Why do you want to strangle me,
this life you see here, who never
caused you injury or insult?

HUNTER.

The Queen hates you. She bid me here
to kill. Ferociously she drove
me to it with her sweet kisses.

QUEEN.

Ha, ha, with kisses, ha, ha, ha.

SNOW WHITE.

Is anything amiss, dear Queen?

QUEEN.

Nothing, play on. You're doing just fine.

PRINCE.

The villain does the villain's role
like second nature. It fits him
as tight as his hunter's costume.

QUEEN.

Prince, Prince!

HUNTER (*to* SNOW WHITE).

Now then, prepare yourself to die.
Don't give me any trouble, please.
You're just sand in the Queen's eyes.
You must leave this beautiful world.
This she wills, this she bid me do.
Be done! Why are you drawing back?

SNOW WHITE.

Can't I fight off this brazen death
when it's grabbing me by my throat?
Are you death, O hard-hearted man!
I don't believe it. You look kind.
A sweet nature dwells on your brows.
You kill beasts, you don't kill people
who're not your open enemy.
I do see this. Mercy makes you
put the knife back. Thank you, thank you!
Would but the Queen have your nature.

QUEEN.

Well, aren't you all holy serious?*
Did you forget and speak the truth?—

* An ironic play on the ideal of holy seriousness (heiliger Ernst) from Goethe's *Wilhelm Meister's Apprenticeship*.

Then, Hunter, please step from this role.
It's unbefitting such a man.
Run the evil whore through, right now.
For the entire afternoon
she's been hectoring me with her
two-faced blathering. O slay her.
Bring that lying heart of hers here
and lay it down at your Queen's feet.

HUNTER *points his dagger at* SNOW WHITE.

PRINCE.
What, what is going on? Snow White, run.
Stop that you, you villain. O Queen,
what a snake you are after all.

QUEEN (*laughing at* HUNTER *while staying his arm*).
All of this is only a game.
Come into the garden. Spring air,
rising, falling in the park's shade,
chatting along the gravelled path,
is the bickering's happy end.
I must be a snake in your eyes,
nothing but evil. No matter,
for the next hour will prove to you
that I am not. Snow White, come.
Prince, if you will allow me now,
I shall call her my dear child.
We were just pretending before!
Trust me, and you played your parts well.
That was just for fun, a dagger
waved around in a hunter's hand.

So he's the villain—ha, ha, ha.
Come, come all into the garden.

PRINCE.

But I still don't quite trust you yet.

QUEEN.

Come, little rabbit Prince! Come too,
Hunter. Laughter shall lead the way.

HUNTER.

Indeed, my Queen.

They exit.

Change of scene.
A garden like the one in the first scene.
QUEEN *and* SNOW WHITE *enter.*

QUEEN.

You lament again as before,
are bitter and give me this sad look.
Why such a change without a word?
You know I don't hold any grudge.
You have no reason to be sad.
Once more the Prince has turned to you
in love anew and yet you sulk
and don't notice that love draws near,
approaches you from every side.

SNOW WHITE.

Oh, but the thought of you hating
and pursuing me I can't shed.
In my troubled mind it follows
me and never, so long as I live,
can I get this out of my mind.

It sticks like this black in my heart.
It darkens every joyful note
of my soul and I am so tired.
I long for that open coffin,
laid out as this frozen image.
Were I but with my dwarfs, then
I would have peace and give you yours.
I plague you. I see you want me
a thousand miles away from here.

QUEEN.

No, no.

SNOW WHITE.

Ah, if I could be with the dwarfs.

QUEEN.

How was it there? Nice and quiet?

SNOW WHITE.

There sleep lays as still as the snow.
If only I could be with them,
those who were as nice as brothers
to me, there where it is sparkling
of this cleanliness that's bracing.
Pain, like some foul leftover food
unpleasant to a refined taste,
was strange to that world's white table.
Like a bedsheet, the happiness
was so clean you fell into sleep,
into this realm of coloured dreams.
And unknown there among those folk
was any ungenerous nature.
Each cherished their gentility,

good manners. Sweet conversations
found upon their lips a response.
I would still be there, but I was
driven in tears to you again,
back into this world where a heart
has to wither away and die.

QUEEN.

So among your dwarfs hate did not
exist? Perhaps love did not too,
was something entirely foreign.
As you know, hate nourishes love,
and love loves not the least of which,
as you well know, cold, bitter hate.

SNOW WHITE.

I never felt a harsh word there.
Hate never tarnished love. If love
was there, that I don't really know.
Hate makes love perceptible first.
There I didn't know what love was.
Here I know, for there's just hate here.
My yearning for love had made me
conscious of love. Inspired by hate,
a soul longs to find love in some place.
And there it dwelt among the dwarfs
in unadulterated joy.
No more about it. That was then.

QUEEN.

Now then, my dear, let's have a laugh.

SNOW WHITE.

No, laughter wants a delight
other than what is in my breast.
My delight is only to cry.
With kisses and flattery
you goaded the Hunter just now,
spurred him on to murder. You said,
'Run the evil whore through,' shaking
with anger. You called it a game.
O, how the desire for revenge
drove your outrageous game with me,
she who knows not how to fight back.
Lower me into my grave. Then
Snow White's grave is Snow White's delight.
I only find delight smiling
in my coffin. There lies my joy.
Lay me with it, O be so kind.

QUEEN.

Now you smile, indeed, you're laughing.

SNOW WHITE.

Ah, if only for a moment.
This other thing tells me once more
about the pain and woe you cause.
It wags with its finger, points long,
and shows me with enormous eyes
what you're up to. Then it whispers,
'Your mother is not your mother.'
The world is never a sweet world.
Love is a leery, wordless hate.
A hunter's a prince. Life is death.

You are not a good queen, rather
you are a proud and wanton one
who dispatched my bloody Hunter.
He's dear to you. You flattered him.
You granted him that one sweet kiss
with which you drove him to the kill.
I am his quarry—all of this
speaks of the next bitter moment.
Now you shall hate me twice over.

QUEEN.

I set him on fire with kisses.
Didn't I? Isn't that so? Say it!
Shout it loud in this gentle world,
into the winds and echo it
into the clouds. Carve it likewise
into these tree trunks rank with leaves,
breathe it into these gentle airs
that they, with this subtle fragrance,
will spread it likewise into spring.
O, then everyone sucks it up,
praising you as the innocent,
calling me the terrible one,
for I fed this murder with love,
inflamed it with a poison kiss.
Hey there, Hunter, where'd you go? Come.
Leave this guilt behind. I'll kiss you,
call you the dearest man of all,
the best, the truest, the strongest and
the handsomest, the boldest man.
Snow White, help me here in my praise.

SNOW WHITE.

Enough, enough, you are going mad.
Had I only not opened up
the poisoned wound. Now it's bleeding
fresh again and will never heal.
If you would but forgive me, Queen.

QUEEN.

To hell with forgiveness, guilt, shame,
going soft. Hey, my faithful servant!

HUNTER *appears.*

HUNTER.

Did you call, Your Highness?

QUEEN.

My one and only, let's kiss first.
I could die. However, I still
should have this short conversation.
I still need to explain this game,
otherwise she, whom it involves,
will call it rude. Talk in my place.
Explain to this silly, sad-eyed girl here
that I do hate and love her too.
Show your dagger. No don't, darling!
Just let it remain in its sheath.
You should only talk, comfort her,
tell her something she can believe,
and reassure me, make it all
peaceful again as it had been
before this casual game began.
Now let's get on with it, and do

watch yourself. Don't say too little
lest your spare words not say too much.

HUNTER.

Snow White, come over here to me.

SNOW WHITE.

Since I'm no longer scared, gladly.

HUNTER.

Do you think I want to kill you?

SNOW WHITE.

Yes and yet no. If I choke Yes,
No swiftly tells me yes again.
I say it so I can believe,
so Yes must ever believe you.
No leaves me tired. Yes is lovely.
I believe you, what you say, too,
I gladly say: Yes, I believe.
No has long been averse to me.
Thus, yes, yes, I do believe you.

HUNTER.

Now see, that's the voice of Snow White.
She's not herself when suspicious,
but a baiter baiting herself
and those who are devotedly
in love with her. Let me say now,
this suspicion just tells a lie,
a made-up, poisonous lie, so,
Snow White, believe me. It's not true!

SNOW WHITE.

Yes, how gladly so. O yes, why
not yes to all that you say.
Saying yes feels so good, is so
endlessly sweet. I believe you.
Yes, if you were to lie, to build
the fairy tale into the sky,
tell me lies, draw me a picture
within reach crudely, awkwardly,
I would believe you for ever.
Yes I must say, for ever yes.
Never has such beautiful faith
swelled in me than now, never such
a sweet confession than this yes.
Say what you want. I believe you.

HUNTER.

How easy you make this business
for me, for you, and this dear Queen.
For that, thanks. But believe me, girl,
bold-faced I've been lying to you.
For the sake of my mistress here,
I tell nothing but fairy tales.

SNOW WHITE.

No, no, don't tell lies to yourself.
I know that it's your soul that speaks.
I trust you. O, such confidence
is safe, has never trusted wrong.
Speak lies. My confidence makes them
into truth as pure as silver.
In fact, I can predict them all.

Whatever you think and say,
this yes will press truth on your words.
Speak, for me, ever faithful,
yes is this prisoner and longs
to be free of his stifling cell.

HUNTER.

I speak then free of guilt and shame
here for the Queen. Do you believe?

SNOW WHITE.

Do I believe this? Yes, why should
I not believe in so much love?
I believe. Be off. I believe.
Just very happily be off.

HUNTER.

That she drove me to this misdeed
with fiery kisses isn't true.
The fairy tale lies, which thus speaks.

SNOW WHITE.

How could it be true since you say
it's not. Be off, I believe.

HUNTER.

That she hates you like a snake,
desirous of your sweet beauty
is a lie. She's a beauty too,
like a resplendent summer tree.
Behold her and call her lovely.

SNOW WHITE.

Lovely, O how lovely. Spring's lush
splendour is hardly so gorgeous.

She surpasses in grandeur
an image of polished marble
when sculpted by a true artist.
She is sweet like a gentle dream.
The fancy of a fevered brow
could not form such a fairy scene.
And how can she be so jealous
of me who stands like the winter
at her side, so frosty and cold?
I don't believe it. How could she?
Go on then, you see, in this case,
I am of the same mind as you.

HUNTER.

Beauty hates beauty not as much
as the fairy tale stated here.

SNOW WHITE.

No, she's surely lovely herself.—
So why hate this sister image,
one who is begging at her feet
and asks that, in the same shadow,
it might exist in her imminence?

HUNTER.

That I wanted to kill you is
an endless childish fantasy.
I never had the heart for it.
From the very start I was touched
by this sad, sweet, childlike pleading
spoken by both your mouth and eyes.
I lowered my dagger and arm,
lifted you up, my sweet, to me.

The deer, which had leapt in our path,
I stabbed myself. Isn't that so?

SNOW WHITE.

I hardly see it worth the time
to bear out this story. Why, yes,
of course. So it was. Yes, indeed.

HUNTER.

The Queen never dispatched poison
intended for you to your dwarfs.
The poison apple isn't true.
The lie that says so is poison.
Even she who makes such claim has
ripened like a beautiful fruit,
tempting, blandishing with splendour,
but inside it would sicken who
is bold enough to taste it.

SNOW WHITE.

It's a lie, black and fantastic,
repugnant to hear, for scaring
children with. Be gone with this lie.
Are you joking? I beg of you,
wring another stupid lie's neck
that just tries to be so clever.
Why is the Queen so quiet?

HUNTER.

She contemplates vain misery.
She thinks of the mistake that plunged
you both in flames of vicious strife.
She weeps for so much confusion.

If I may ask, Snow White, kiss her,
anything that would express love.

SNOW WHITE (*kisses her*).

Then permit me this sweet token.
See how pale you are! Forgive me
if I take your pallor's life with
these kisses. See, they sponge it up,
every bit of this tragic hue
that would so disfigure your bliss.
Hunter, have you nothing newer?

HUNTER.

O, still so much, but silence now.
An end kisses in the end, though
a beginning is still not through.
The Queen gives me a gracious nod
and my words choke up in her grace.
As one blessed, I keep my silence.

KING, PRINCE, *ladies-in-waiting and nobles appear.*

SNOW WHITE.

O good Father, with your august
seal press on that not-yet-smothered
strife between these two burning hearts.
Accept my kiss, and trample out
this jealous strife into the ground
as an emissary of peace.

KING.

I always thought you peaceable.
What kind of strife, my lovely child?

QUEEN.

No more strife, just a smiling word,
a jest taking a serious mien
which tricks you with a looming brow.
There was some strife here, but no more.
Love knew how to win here. Hate
perished in such a stronger love.
I did hate—it was just a game,
a tantrum taken much too far,
the bluster of a passing mood.
No more than that. Now it's sweet peace.
For a while a wounded envy
felt it had to hate. Ah, that hurt
myself more than anyone else.
Snow White here can affirm me.

KING.

Is the Hunter blameless? The Prince
here bitterly accuses him.

SNOW WHITE.

Pureness points to heaven no more.
Perhaps you believe he trafficked
in illicit love with the Queen,
exchanging kiss and embrace, O,
don't believe that. You are deceived
by the temperament of this man,
which is as precious as a gem.
Love must cherish him, honour crown
him beyond doubt. Brave man, to whom
more gratitude than gratitude
can ever owe, I repay you.

(*To* KING) Lord, everything is peaceable,
and strife looks just like a blue sky.

KING.

Here indeed then a miracle
has happened during this short hour.

PRINCE.

The villain is villain no more.

QUEEN.

Hush, noble Prince, it's ignoble,
such a weakness for minor faults,
in the scene you keep pointing out
whose blossoming you yourself sought,
not blanket him up. Were he great,
we'd not now be standing gathered
so peacefully. Give me your hand,
forget the guilt in a friend's squeeze.

PRINCE.

I should forget that here is this
confounded poisonous villain,
the green knave in the hunting clothes,
who for but a short hour courted
such rich favour from the Queen?
Make me forget that I am an
anointed prince and a ruler,
but not this sin, which is too great
for just any oblivion.

SNOW WHITE.

O, there's no longer any sin.
It's no longer in this circle.

It's fled from us. The sinner here,
I, as her true child, kiss her hand
and ask of her if she might but
sin as much in so dear a way.
Why, Prince, why do you stir up strife?
Have you forgotten what you swore
only but a short while ago?
Did you not swear love to the Queen,
kneel for her beautiful image
of devotion and sweet splendour?
Show now love, it truly befits
you best to joyfully render
the homage here of a shy kiss.
I, too, I thought I had been hurt,
the one harmed, hated and cast out.
How stupid and stubborn I was
alike to see an evil sin,
to hastily trust in mistrust
and be so blind in bitterness.
Cast off the rash prejudice of
condemnation and fierce justice.
Justice is this clemency here,
and clemency is peace enwreathed,
part of this sweet, blessed revel
that tosses sin into the air,
plays with it as with the flowers.
Be happy you can be happy.
O, could I speak. I must too
for such a great and blessed end.
But I lack that gift for eloquence.

Passion is much too wild in me
and I am so intensely filled
by such lofty, contrary joy.

QUEEN.

Oh, but how sweet you speak, fair child!

KING.

Take this kiss, and may all have
a fete of royal joy this day.
Prince, you'd be better served if you
fell in with the joy shared by all.
You don't want to be a stranger
and apart from such faithfully
devoted, heartfelt happiness.
What? Why do you still look angry?

PRINCE.

Not angry, and not liking it.
I just don't know what I should say.

PRINCE *exits.*

QUEEN (*to* SNOW WHITE).

And are you no longer tired now?
You want to laugh again, have fun
and spread cheer as if it were seed?

SNOW WHITE.

I'm tired no more. What? Did the Prince
run in fear from our rejoicing?
Does this befit this noble man?

QUEEN.

Sure it befits—he's a coward!

SNOW WHITE.

I don't know if he's a coward.
But such conduct was bad of him.
Go, Hunter, bring him back here.

HUNTER *exits.*

I want to scold him when he comes,
and he'll surely come. He just wants
us anxiously looking for him.

QUEEN.

Then he will still be your sweetheart.
And then—then I say, yes indeed,
must say something I remember, say—
What do I say? Ah, yes, then say,
something like this perchance, saying:
'You fired him on with your kisses
to that—'

SNOW WHITE.

Hush, O hush. Just the fairy tale
says so, not you and never me.
I said it just once, once like that—
it's over and done. Father, come.
Lead the way inside for us all.

All go towards the castle.

THORN ROSE, OR THE SLEEPING BEAUTY

(1920)

THORN ROSE.

You, you who stand in this circle,
please take a good look at this man.
He woke me from my hundred years
of deep sleep and so he wishes
to now take me to be his wife.

KING.

He will wish he was not so bold.
What's he done that is important?

THORN ROSE.

He came by this way and kissed me,
and with this kiss he woke me up.

FIRST LADY-IN-WAITING.

Anybody could just as well.

QUEEN.

Surely he has freed the castle
and lifted the spell over us,

yet that, I would hope, should hardly
warrant such a desire as his.

KING.

I would hope too,

SECOND LADY-IN-WAITING.

me too,

THORN ROSE.

me too.

KING.

Say, good stranger, can you give fair
proof of exactly who you are too?

THORN ROSE.

Does he not have eyes like the sea,
a countenance like marble
and a deportment like granite?
Well, I wouldn't like such a man.
Let him find another sweetheart.

THIRD LADY-IN-WAITING.

Above all, should he not behave
a little friendlier? He stands
like a fence post and doesn't move.
Nor has his mouth opened either.
Hey? Can you say something or not?

STRANGER.

I will speak of things soon enough.
There's really no terrible rush.

KING.

He awakened us from our sleep
and seems quite still asleep himself.

GROUNDSKEEPER.

This service that he has performed
is rather doubtful and he could
have easily spared himself
all this trouble for our sake.
Wasn't it lovely just to sleep?
Were we not so much better off?

COACHMAN.

If I still slept, I'd not have to climb
on my box now and be bothering
with those stubborn, stamping horses.

COOK.

If I still slept, I would not now
have to fight with the scullion maids.

SCULLERY MAID.

And I wouldn't have to pluck chickens,

MAMSELLE.*

and I wouldn't have to fluff the pillows,

SERVANT.

I would not have to shine these shoes.

HUNTER.

The game would be sleeping like me
had this monsieur here not come around.

ACCOUNTANT.

The books would no longer be a bane,
I'd never need to settle accounts,
balances would be little bother.

* A chambermaid.

COURT POET.

If I were asleep, no verses
would have to be laboured over.
I'd still be lying on my ear
and dreaming of nothing but fame.
Now I'll wrestle around for rhymes,
earning nothing but ingratitude.
I would rather he had remained
in his cuckoo nest or somewhere
that suited him and let us sleep.
This was no masterstroke on his part.

MINISTER.

If only I were still asleep.
I would not be taxing my brain
with such difficult alliances.

GOVERNESS.

Must I warn the children all over
to be on their best behaviour now?
Perhaps no one thinks of what a world
of trouble this is going to cost me.

PROFESSOR.

Science and scholarship for my sake
could have still continued slumbering
peacefully a little while longer.

FIRST LADY-IN-WAITING.

Anyway, he surely claims credit
for his having accomplished something.
If only he had graced someone else
with his presence sooner instead
and had been willing to spare us it.

THORN ROSE.

But there he is now after all.

KING.

Sadly, yes.

THORN ROSE.

Say, how'd you get here?
Don't you have eyes like the ocean?
Did the waves toss you ashore here?
Did you fall from the clouds to us?

STRANGER.

Did I come so undesired then?

THORN ROSE.

So as to disturb my pleasant dream.

STRANGER.

Isn't reality a dream too?
Aren't we all, even when awake,
going about something like dreamers,
sleepwalkers in the light of day,
who but play with what comes to mind
and act as though awake?
Well, we are, but what is being awake?
Does some god lead us by the hand?
Would he not do so where we have gone?
Have we any guarantee that we
would survive without someone on high?
Could we stand this test without support
such that we would not know about it,
because it's a riddle to us?
All is a dream, our houses are,

trade, industry, our daily sustenance,
the cities, the countries and the
light and the sun. No one can claim
he understands. Understanding
is but piecemeal, never otherwise.

KING.

Just give us the facts.

STRANGER.

As you know,
I felt bored at my father's court.
So one day I just wandered away
to see for myself what they call life,
and when I felt myself getting tired,
I slept where I could on the hard ground,
and afterwards I walked once more,
and if someone stood in my way,
I fought for myself. Then I heard
about you.

THORN ROSE.

About me?

STRANGER.

They said
you slept in a tower surrounded
by wild roses and thorns, that you
were under a spell. Only he who
broke through to you could rescue you.

THORN ROSE.

That whetted your curiosity.

STRANGER.

Perhaps I felt like taking the risk.
I continued on my journey
without ever having seen you,
just you in spirit before me,
with me every step of the way.
At twilight, I would spend the time
thinking of how gentle you were and
sweet, and how wonderful it would be
to wake you, for me to look upon
you a little, to draw you towards me
tighter and tighter and you thinking
of me, that I am good enough.
Perhaps I stand here somewhat awkward.
Something, however, happens as I
stand here in the flesh, as well I do.
So I wandered on and then came here,
walked without any long second thoughts
into this enveloping rankness,
which, like it knew the time had come,
pulled away its thorns then and there
such that I found unobstructed
an entrance and hastened to you.
I saw and kissed you. Then you opened
your eyes,

THORN ROSE.

because I had been surprised
by such a bold intruder?

STRANGER.

Many,
of those who weren't as lucky as me,
I saw lying on the ground. A few
seemed to be smiling, as if they
were content in death to have achieved
this tempting prize.

THORN ROSE.

Those poor men, O those
valiant souls who risked life with disdain,
who beheld what seemed more beautiful,
who crumbled away exemplary,
who had conquered both love and honour,
who had lived less worthy and less brave.
I will think about this all my life
and the thought shall be bracing to me,
like a flower's fragrance. I would be
awful if I did not think of it
continually as though it were
my own breath.

STRANGER.

How true, how true, and I'm
plainly embarrassed at my success
to stand before you—

THORN ROSE.

where so many
good men had to die, who fervently
desired me just as much as you,
who with blue-flashing eyes and blond hair,
with unsullied courage, with their young

breasts full of youthful compulsion
to snatch from life its passion, had vied
for me—you alone touched what fate
would not grant them. We struggle
in vain when it won't, even when
giants take our cause. Lady Fortune!
Pooh! For a moment there, I was
almost becoming annoyed. Well, look
now! I am beginning to believe
you have a right to me and it's the right thing
that I belong to you now.

QUEEN.

Don't you want to think this step through?
Think about what you're saying here.

THORN ROSE.

Were I to think it over longer,
I could spoil it for me in the end.
No, I am entirely in agreement
with myself, and he is my lord now.
Still, I would rather see my hero
otherwise, as a lot more handsome,
somewhat more pleasing and elegant,
more charming too, and in a certain
sense more proud. But, alas, I cannot
say these things. I must accept him now, as
he is, and do so sincerely.

STRANGER.

I am your gallant servant always!
And should I but only half please you,
should you have to all but force yourself

to see, to love and to suffer me,
let me tell you a French proverb now:
*L'appétit vient en mangeant.** I hope
that I shall succeed in pleasing you.

THORN ROSE.

So be it! Now let there be music
and let's all be happy together.
The sun is shining and the sky is
looking blue, and winds are fanning us
with a breeze unabashedly cool.
This palace is now coming to life.
And going forwards every one of us
will cheerfully challenge ourselves
and eagerly help where there is need,
with our eyes looking bright and living
happy as one and in such a way
that all things considered we shall build
towards a flourishing companionship.

KING.

Because what you say, child, isn't bad,
count me in,

QUEEN.

me too,

STRANGER.

and me too
because it can't happen otherwise.

* Appetite comes with the eating.

THORN ROSE.

Me too, for clearly without me
it does not happen.

STRANGER.

No, it does not.

THORN ROSE.

But it can happen—

STRANGER.

yes, yes, it can.

THORN ROSE.

The longer we talk, the colder
our soup gets, so let's break off here
and together go to dinner.
May I please have your arm?

EVERYONE.

Thus the matter came pleasantly
to an end with a joyful wedding.

PART IV

Later Dramolettes

THE CHRIST CHILD

(1920)

JOSEPH.

What goes on inside this cottage?
Who are these strange people I see?
What a curious gathering!
In the weak glow of my lantern,
I can make out all kinds of faces.
Who are you? Where do you come from
and what would make you turn out here?
Speak!

YOUNG GIRL.

I can hardly explain why.
I'd rather you didn't ask me.
I only heard that here on this night
something glorious would happen
and thought I'd like to be here too,
even though I am but a poor,
scorned girl.

SOLDIER.

Did they not say,
the Long-Awaited One would be born?

OLD MAN.

I heard something to that effect too.

JOSEPH.

Who says so?

SOLDIER.

I don't know.

YOUNG GIRL.

Nor do I.

JOSEPH.

But who are these worthy gentlemen
in discussion among themselves?
They appear to be of a high rank,
as shown by their sumptuous garments.
All this cultured bearing of theirs
is too plain for me to take them
to be mere humble folk.

FIRST KING.

We are
potentates from the Orient.
Some give us the title of wise men.
To others we appear as kings.

JOSEPH.

Is that so? Well, that's fine by me.
It's a shame that I can't wait on you
with something.

SECOND KING.

We thank you from our hearts,
but we don't need anything at all.
Our being here is refreshment enough.

JOSEPH.

Is it possible that you made
such a long journey just to come
and meet a simple carpenter?
I can hardly understand why.
Take no offence on my account.

THIRD KING.

It may well indeed have been God
who gave us a sign to follow,
to come here, inside this cramped space,
where lies that little boy, the one
who shall one day redeem mankind.

JOSEPH.

How did you come by this wonderful
idea? It almost frightens me.
Of course, a child has been born here,
but hardly for such a lofty
purpose.

SOLDIER.

Show it to us.

JOSEPH.

If you would
like to see it now, take a quick look
around. It lies there in the corner
by his mother.—And this fellow, you're
in awe too?

JESTER.

Incredibly so!

VAGANBOND.

I too would very much like to see
this miracle child.

JOSEPH.

Your glimpse is
granted you. Come, closer.

All step towards the child.

This is it!

MARY.

Who are these people you talk to?

JOSEPH.

They would like to see our baby.
They say—

MARY.

Well, what do they say then?

JOSEPH.

It's the Messiah.

MARY.

What? This child?

JOSEPH.

Yes, and it was born for the sake
of the rapture of all humankind.

MARY.

Have they been taken in by deceit?

JOSEPH.

Honestly, they just don't give me
that impression given the way

they are too polite, they speak much
too thoughtfully. Talk to them yourself.

MARY.

You're most welcome. Thank you so much
for your company and kind faces,
and for being nice enough to have
asked us.

SHEPHERD.

Room for one or two more
might be found in this cubbyhole.

JOSEPH.

This crowd is getting rather large.
But I shall not bar you entry.
Instead, let me wish you a warm
good evening and ask that you make
yourselves at home as best you can.

SHEPHERD.

Outside all was silent, but for
singing from the starry sky: 'Christ is
risen!' I thought I must see him
and now I realize this is it.

SOLDIER.

It's him.

JOSEPH.

You have such perfect faith,
I might end up being a believer
myself.

MARY.

Aren't you always a child,
this despite your years and many
lessons learnt? Do you want your beard
to laugh at you and those wrinkles
on your brow to feel shame? Don't talk
so carelessly.

JOSEPH.

I'll bear that in mind.
After all, it is vain of me
to believe such a thing of this child,
like it was the future Messiah.

YOUNG GIRL.

Why is such an enchanted glow
shining around the face of him?
From where comes this lovely shaft of light?
Or do my eyes play tricks on me?

OLD MAN.

No, no, I see the glow now too.
If the whole room's not bright with it,
I'm blinded by an evil mirage.

SOLDIER.

Yes, I see it too, and all can see,
and all mankind to come will find
this hour precious. Will he not draw
everyone to him, who does not yet
talk, but will one day speak of things
divine? I am his prisoner
and now regret all my past deeds.

I marched through Galilee, Egypt,
Syria. I left my regiment
to greet this child. What a deep joy
transfixes me before his image.
I never trembled before danger,
me, the one who hurt so many.
I've never shown any feeling
when they cried out that I spare them.
Now what do I feel? Do I dream?
Am I no longer the same man?
Am I now another person,
Someone higher?

OLD MAN.

No, one more gentle,
and of course someone higher too.
As you revere this tender young life,
I, an old man, shall do so too.
Have I, for as long as I've lived,
seen a more beautiful moment?
Have I ever known, as the whole world
must by now, such a joyous event,
such great hope? Some day it will be said
this was the time when love and faith
were born.

JOSEPH.

Don't you go on and on,
almost like a boy or well-nigh
more. What is all this spirit for
on this night?

MARY.

Perhaps they're all either
quite mad or simply too overjoyed.
Could it be that God speaks from their mouths?

JOSEPH.

Would I know? I gave it no thought.
I've hardly seen anything odd
in these occurrences, not till
they said there is a miracle here.
Now that has me shaking my head.
You know that I am, if anything,
a sensible man, someone who's
sober and thinks practically.
This childlike appearance, I myself
didn't take it all too much to heart.
'Well, it's a child like any other.
Hopefully, he'll turn out just fine.'
This is pretty much how I thought.
Now I'm nearly bewildered by their
dreamy talk, as though I had indulged
in a heady drink. Still, I trust
in God.

MARY.

Which is for the best too.
I'm pleased by how upright you are,
humble and good, as it should be.

ONE OF THE KINGS.

Let us kneel before the child
and lay our gifts before him here
at his feet.

The KINGS *kneel.*

JOSEPH.

Worthy gentlemen,
aren't you being a bit too polite?
Don't you think you're being much too nice
to me and my wife, to such plain
and simple people as we are?

FIRST KING.

It's for showing our devotion,
and for this joyous arrival.
If anything, it's just the way
we decorate things. Such objects,
as precious as they may seem to you,
we have all over the place. So
don't tell us how grateful you are.
You've given us more, for we will
bring this joy back to our homeland,
for we have seen the Messiah,
the Lord, in whom many people
will one day have faith and build him
a temple. However, he will
not be so fortunate himself
as one might think.

MARY.

What do you mean?

SECOND KING.

A smart man says nothing at all,
neither what he knows nor what he
thinks he might know.

FIRST KING.

You're right.
(*To* MARY) I meant
only that your son, so great in love,
could be like in suffering, nothing
that might give you cause to worry.

MARY.

Even as you give me joy, now you
give me a heavy heart.

THIRD KING.

It's nothing.
He talks a bit too much.
(*To his colleague*) Better
if you could keep it to yourself.

MARY.

Suffering? Am I beginning
to see what fate lies in store for my son?
You look at me as though you cared
for me, as though concerned, but what
you're telling me doesn't sound pleasant.

JOSEPH.

Peace and love and faith as well, go
above all else.

MARY.

Of course, you good
man.

JOSEPH.

While it seems a trifle gloomy,

things will soon be cheerful once more.
We don't want to let our hearts get
any sadder. After all, God has
given this child to you, thus will
He lead it by the hand as well
through this unforeseeable life.

OLD MAN.

How serious everything is.

JESTER.

Shall we be off?

VAGABOND.

Someone surely
should make a start. Joy and sorrow,
greatness and baseness, are ever
cheek by jowl. This bit of wisdom
comes from a good-for-nothing's head.

JOSEPH.

Good night!

SOLDIER.

I'll be off too. Good night!

THIRD KING.

We'll be wanting to go to our inn.

OLD MAN.

I should probably be going too.

YOUNG GIRL.

And I should do the same. Sleep well!

JOSEPH.

Well, they have all gone away now.

MARY.

Should we sleep too, like the others?
Surely you're a little tired from
talking to our guests. They gave you
so many things to think about.

JOSEPH.

Of course I'm a little sleepy,
but I'd rather you slept alone
and let me keep watch, so the child,
who they tell us is so special,
doesn't lack a faithful guardian.
Just close your eyes. Mine shall remain
open, so that nothing befalls
this gentleness, so that your dreams
are sweet and pleasant, with their shapes
calmly, lovingly wrapped around you.
Do not the stars watch outside too,
above our hill, this eternal soul
which is the spirit of the world,
which is this universe, this one
which never sleeps. Listen, who knocks
there at the door?

ANGEL.

You may lie
down, one mightier will keep watch.

JOSEPH.

I'll do what you tell me.

ANGEL.

Then you
do well.

JOSEPH.

Will this child be cared for?

ANGEL.

Be without worry, what you love,
and who loves you, if you be true,
rest easy, thus should you too.

JOSEPH.

Good night!

MARY.

My faith is finally
restored. Some day, when everything
is not as nice as I would like
to think, maybe this way I'll have
the strength to bear it.

JOSEPH.

So sleep well.

ANGEL.

It's a very curious thing
about the apprehensive minds
of mortals, as though they always
want to flee what's been decided
on high, ever wanting to believe,
putting everything in order,
making extra work for themselves.
Yet it is the good and the kind
who do so, who don't want to rest,
for they think they will miss something.
The Lord has dispatched me hither,
so that I stand vigilant guard.

It seems He holds both of them dear
such that He'll spare them having to know.
Surely something special is in store
for the little child, otherwise
He'd not care so for the parents.
Will He endow it with wisdom
and beauty, prepare it for life's
journey, which is aglow with great
suffering, and then the heavy test,
to claim for itself its divine,
lofty, eternal dwelling place?

THE LOVERS

(1921)

In a salon.

OSKAR.

Look, what is it with people here?
How solemnly they walk about.
This one carries himself with force,
and that one over there, stooped and shy.
There are quite a few here for whom
I would almost feel some pity.
Oh, everything is of two minds,
so arid and hard. I think that
people could be ten times gentler,
nicer, more conscientious, courteous,
when it actually matters for once.
Politeness and some good manners
do not amount to good company,
do not make a decent party.
No matter how sincere they are,
they are strangers. I have such an
incredible need to leave here

tomorrow morning. Want to go?
Would you like that? Coming with me?

EMMA.

Since it's you encouraging me,
then I shall do so willingly.
Indeed, I believe in you as
I do in light, resolute to much
harder things than going for a stroll
together with you.

OSKAR.

How happy
you make me with your acquiescence.

EMMA.

And you me the more with your dear
belief in me.

OSKAR.

And you the more
with your courage.

EMMA.

And you the more
with everything that you are.

OSKAR.

Does life not lie like a garden
before us, and don't you too feel
the world's beauty?

EMMA.

If I did not,
how could you possibly stand me?
Could you befriend a little doll?

OSKAR.

No, I can't.

EMMA.

Nor I, were I you.

A forest.

OSKAR.

Is it not lovely here?

EMMA.

It's quiet,
like being in a temple. Are the pines
not almost like columns and the moss-
covered ground not unlike a rug?
The most wondrous flowers grow here.
I'd love to pick them one by one,
but I can't be she who disturbs
such tender existences. It means
wilfully defiling this forest.
Such a thing is so far from me.

OSKAR.

How this splendour surrounds us here,
and yet even the tiniest leaf
asserts itself. There's nothing here
which should be concealed from our view.
The beetle may bestir itself,
and the ants go this way and that,
and from this heavenliness sunlight
rains down, and outside there plays
the wind. Listen to the train there
in the distance, where people travel

as well. We are here with rabbits,
with squirrels, and butterflies, with
us alone.

EMMA.

What do we do when night falls?

OSKAR.

We will simply lie down someplace
and sleep on the ground, as though we
were at home and wanted to slip
into bed.

On a secluded mountaintop.

EMMA.

I wish I were a bit less tired;
how quickly our strength disappears!

OSKAR.

Shall I go fetch you some water?
Perhaps I'll find a spring around here.

EMMA.

No, stay. I'll be fine. Let's just rest.
I'm so ashamed of my weakness!
As soon as the body weakens,
the soul follows and then gives up hope.
Oh, that we have to eat and drink
and never eat and drink our fill
of beauty. How high the swallows fly.
I would love to live in that sea
of air! Those magnificent clouds!
It's not for us. We're too heavy

for that, and yet the thought of it
invigorates us, and we feel
strong by merely being aware. Is
that not a house there? Possibly
we could get a drop of milk there.
Where is my sense of adventure?
I can barely go on.

OSKAR.

Maybe I was a little careless,
taking you, so tender a thing, here.

A house.

EMMA.

All is silent, and nothing save flies
buzz, and nothing but the sunshine
lives here.

OSKAR.

The house is utterly empty,
the walls are black, as if there was
a fire. Not a sound, just a few
things left behind. No furniture,
and no one to ask us what is
our business here. In the kitchen
nothing's been cooked for a long time.

EMMA.

Is someone sleeping there?

OSKAR.

No, it's just
a log. Let's go.

EMMA.

How I long for
people suddenly.

OSKAR.

Perhaps we might
meet someone who can tell us where
a town lies.

They come to a town.

OSKAR.

Girls are at play and the pigeons
flutter. Austerely garbed women
walk about. There's a gentle stream
here and a bridge over it. Entire
families in the open air, young
and old, poor and rich, a little dog
walks behind a lady. The bells
toll—the shapes and the masonry,
buildings and houses standing here
for centuries and yet so solid
they seem erected yesterday.
See the palace with its statues,
how it stands proud, vast and brittle!
Think of everything which already
happened inside. Through the open
windows, people are looking down
at life, as if they were sitting
in a theatre and just watching a play.
Their being purely spectators has
made them utterly lifeless. There is

just the sky above the streets, here
narrow, there broad. In the restaurants
they drink beer, they talk politics,
play cards or flirt with the waitress.
Does that person there want something
from us? He watches us.

THE STRANGER.

I am
just a wandering carpenter,
and if you could spare anything,
I would wish you a good long life
and health without end, the reason
being that I'm terribly thirsty
and would love just a little to go
inside that inn there.

EMMA.

Give him something.
He speaks sincerely and openly.
I do love such simple people.
They still go through the world, carrying
the good old days around with them.

In front of a church.

EMMA.

The door is open so anyone
can look inside. How beautiful
it is here. The sanctuary
is decorated with paintings.
Someone is praying, and only
two steps away they casually

converse about everyday life.
Here anyone can feel what they want.
There are no orders to follow.
God wants none to believe in him.
He doesn't pressure any soul
for there is nothing about him
to force us. Who doesn't need him,
doesn't see him. He exists for those
who love him, see him and desire
him. Is he not the most lenient,
most gentle being, and benevolent
through and through? About the temple birds
chirp, the fields and meadows are near
and nothing here is unfriendly.
The chaplain speaks to two women.
There's a man of the world about him,
whose engaging gestures gain more
than with intolerance and pride.
He consoles as he jests, and instructs
with a smile for he sees himself
as a plain fellow man. It smells
after all spiritual and nice
and serious at the same time.

At the edge of a gorge.

A POSTCARD VENDOR.

Buy something from an old woman.

OSKAR.

Do you have anything nice?

VENDOR.

Charming postcards,
informative books.

OSKAR.

What is this book? What's it about?

VENDOR.

It's about a poor thief released
from the women's penitentiary,
how she searches for employment,
how she wants honest work again,
but people make her an outcast,
how she sees her little boy once more
and she hugs him close to her heart,
but he wants nothing to do with her
and he runs from her in terror,
how this hurts her and how one night
she dreams of new sins, of sitting
behind iron bars again, of not
suffering it and sooner dying.

OSKAR.

Give me a copy. How much is it?

VENDOR.

Only forty rappen.*

EMMA.

Interested
are you in such things?

* A Swiss penny.

OSKAR (*to* VENDOR).

Are you not
Flückiger's sister?*

VENDOR.

Yes, I am her.

It is evening.

EMMA.

The way all these objects glow now.
The houses and trees and woods are red
from this colourful shaft of light.
Is mankind up on its feet today,
children, grown-ups, all the poor
and good people, the excited
and the overjoyed?

OSKAR.

They are all drawn to the same spot,
and all of them have the same thought.
Were they dead once and now alive?
Oh the way they all seem happy
and stride briskly. Even the tired
move lighter, and all, all of them
are young, as if henceforth there is
only this youth. Has a god dispersed
pettiness, ignobility
and indolence, have we arrived

* Flückiger is a common surname in the Bernese region of Switzerland. Therefore, it could be another play on Swiss sameness and individuality.

at something human? I've yet to
see the ocean, but I see it now.

EMMA.

Does the sun blind us such that we
would want to see what just doesn't
exist?

OSKAR.

Someone stood there and sang
at the window, where all broke loose,
became overwhelming, and then
floated as though into focus
and became the burning present.

EMMA.

No one is here, we have seen things
that exist only in our minds
and in our dreams.

OSKAR.

So where to next?

EMMA.

I had thought that all people longed
to be blissfully happy and walked
in an enormous procession
into the setting sun, to where
a much prettier existence
would blossom, where every path
would be full of devout beings, their
souls turned towards, facing the true.
Now I see nothing but my only
love, you alone, my everything.

A restaurant.
A GENTLEMAN *and a* LADY *talk about a third person.*

LADY.

This would surely benefit him
in every way imaginable.
He should really think about it.

GENTLEMAN.

If he thinks about it for much more,
he is a fool.

LADY.

America
isn't outer space. Many have made
their fortunes there. It would be a shame
for such an opportunity.

GENTLEMAN.

I say he should make use of it.
Send him to me. For eight whole days
I won't say anything to him
but 'Begone'. He should travel.
If he doesn't, something's wrong with him
and he belongs in a nuthouse.
He'll make money like bricks over there,
be manager. What will he do here?
A poor wretch just wasting away.
If I knew he didn't want to go,
I'd go crazy, right out of my mind,
stark raving mad, and have a stroke.
Anyone who could be a made man
and doesn't immediately do
what's necessary to become one

should have a sign hanging from him
that reads: 'I am an ass.' That's my
honest opinion. If he doesn't
take the chance he's as good as
got in the bag, I'll be furious.

LADY.

He'll go. He wants to.

GENTLEMAN.

Don't make me
mad. Your composure has something
unseemly about it. Money,
money, just take it when it's there
for the taking, for goodness sakes!
When it's about making money,
I could care less if it's me or
someone else pocketing it. The point
is that it pays off if anything.
What can a kid like you ever know
about such things? Don't make me laugh.
If he doesn't leave, he doesn't know
what's good for him. Let me have him,
I'll push him until he steams away.
Come on, let's go. Just admit it,
that I'm right? Hey?

They leave.

EMMA.

We have just heard
a pleasant conversation here,
wouldn't you say?

OSKAR.

It could almost prove
the desire for success. Could you love
and respect such a person?

EMMA.

Hardly.

A street, early morning.

OSKAR.

I don't know you, but you almost
look familiar.

WAYFARER.

It may well be,
strangers can seem familiar to one.
I was a soldier, now I march
to India all on my own,
my own responsibility,
my own cost. I'll make this journey
as still as possible, even
if it takes years. I have no binding
contract to be here or be there
where and when, and nobody is
waiting for me, so I am free.
The world and time are vast, generous.
I couldn't stand being dependent.
If I find a job, I'll take it,
and when the work is done, well then,
I'll just keep roaming on, living
in uncertainty, but loving it.
Tight borders would make me anxious.

Only here in the open air
can I find peace, where I feel like
I float along. I have light feet,
I eat very little, something like
wanting to be a monk. While I'm
not so sure about it, it will be
all right in the end. I've nothing
at home, but everything's outside.
So why come to a standstill then?
I like to run as little as I
like to lie, to mourn as little as
to laugh. I love that which remains
the same. Perhaps I would have made
a good scholar, but I would have
to sit still and study. I could
not have done that, so I became
an assistant, who advances
step by step to get where he wants
to be. A soldier will with some
tact and a bit of talent know
how to be helpful anywhere.
I see a tall peak in India
bathed in pink light and in the green
land a house and rivers and many,
many kind and patient people
living off God knows what and lying down
in silence when the time has come,
while we make a big fuss about
life and death. Are we any better
than flowers? And yet no one dares

to think about them. Animals
are unaware of what's right and wrong.
They stare and know nothing. I find
in such naivety something
innocent, paradisiacal.
Oh, what beautiful broadleaf trees,
what meadows, things lovely, delights
that may have existed before,
but there are still beautiful things.
Actually, I can neither love
nor hate anything, neither respect
nor disrespect anything. I live
and survive, so adieu.

He leaves.

OSKAR.

That one
knows not what to like and dislike,
what fortune and misfortune is,
knows no goal, no passion. He is
like the wind and clouds.

EMMA.

Maybe no
heart either?

OSKAR.

Go, ask him.

EMMA.

He's gone,
and he would have given me no
answer.

Moonlit night.

OSKAR.

Do you hear the wind's voice? Up there
they sit and stand high on the cliff
making music. It's enchanting here!
There are lovers who sit on lawns
and park benches. How sweet is love.
How little is it worth, desired,
yet not treasured. It should be worth
more and endure for longer, mean much,
much more, for only it provides
happiness, and being happy
only provides beauty, and only
that which is beautiful is good.
How beautiful the dark makes you!

EMMA.

Yes, they're happy as we are too.
Shall we walk over to those trees?
The fountain purls so intimately.
See how the lake glistens and the
stars shimmer. Is such a night not
like a holy picture?

OSKAR.

Up above
they tell each other who they are,
where they are from, what they do,
how they mean well to one another,
and how they want to be in love
for their entire lives—Oh what joy!—

and speak of nothing but truth, feel
nothing but good. Lovers are true,
they don't care about opinions
and don't need to respect childish
explanations in this stillness.
No one but Cupid can hear them,
nothing can hinder their embracing
and kissing. The gentle night breeze
strokes their hair and faces, like us,
dear Emma.

EMMA.

And what about us, we don't kiss. Why not?

They do.

OSKAR.

They work very hard,
so neither should we be idle,
and what they accomplish, we will
achieve as well.

EMMA.

They are in bliss,
all these lovers who are in love,
who understand each other. Must
we not feel before we understand?
Reason's not enough, how often
it's irrational.

OSKAR.

I am astonished by your wisdom.

EMMA.

It seems you make fun of me now.
Go ahead, a little ridicule
won't hurt.

OSKAR.

If you don't take it wrong.

EMMA.

Let's start walking to those trees now,
where there is less breeze, where there is
dark and quiet. There we will sit
and see if we can be as tender
as the others. It seems perhaps
we'll give ourselves a kiss as sweet
as the others, and love thinking
of the caresses, the happiness
and the joy of others. Shouldn't this make
us still more happy?

Years later. OSKAR *sits in a parlour.*

EMMA (*looking through the window, speaking to herself*).

He does not notice me, hears nothing,
sees nothing, just busy with himself,
just reads and reads, knowing only books,
stuck in this room, day in, day out,
not feeling like looking any more,
no small talk, no thought of hiking.
He's forgotten the paths,
the forests, and people, me
too perhaps. He lost his nice smile,
thinks, contemplates, nothing comes.

Blue skies and bright air no longer
beckon him. He doesn't seem sad.
This reclusiveness pleases him.
He doesn't regret all the hours
he spends in here tight-lipped. I stand
here in vain, he doesn't miss me.
His thoughts, his quests, his fertile mind,
his iron-willed learning are everything
to him. He wants nothing. I could
talk to him, but that would only
annoy him, so I'd rather leave. The
sun, that play
of the light, all this pleasantly
effortless life, all that is soft,
clever is nothing to him. Only
the agitations of the mind
engage him, those delectations
in the realm of thought. He just sits there
seeming almost hunchbacked to me.
His once-slender neck is unsightly.
He has something of a porter
about him and he no longer loves
himself, withdraws from people, pays
no more heed to reality.
He's building something in his head,
only that which he finds worthy
of existence. No more will I
come and go. If he fails to feel
my presence, he won't my absence
either. I can't help him. No one can.

SEDUCER.

What do you want with this homebody?
I mean to be candid with you.
I'm just taken by your beauty.
It's true! And, if you would, let me
provide you with my services.

EMMA (*looks at him, astonished*).

What?

SEDUCER.

I seek some way to make myself
indispensable to you, and that
I think will not be very hard.

EMMA.

Don't flatter yourself.

SEDUCER.

That one
in there cheats on you.

EMMA.

But surely
he would not act so carelessly.

SEDUCER.

He does nevertheless and he has
nothing to even offer you,
the idealist.

EMMA.

What do you want then?

SEDUCER.

To show you that one can be noble
as well as harsh, that another

can be cruel and to some degree
good for you.

EMMA.

And you're proud of this?

SEDUCER.

Beauty that's not so beautiful,
ugliness not so ugly, it's true,
but not as naive souls would think.
I'll introduce you to the world,
I'll open your eyes and escort you
into life itself, for I do see
how much you really long for it.
In short, I wish to cultivate you.

EMMA.

You liar!

SEDUCER.

I am charmed by your
insults. Do you know how I find you
adorable?

EMMA.

Could it be he's
not that unbearable to me?

Both live apart.

OSKAR.

What I had to see in that dream
just now, them with nothing at all
going on, yet not wanting to part,
them being angry, pale and wan,
and them with no hope of ever

winning, looking at each other
with sombre faces, and neither
one could understand the other,
neither could speak of the pleasant
nor of the truth, neither could lie
nor find the strength to be totally
sincere, like snakes these sick people
crawled and bit themselves in two. One
wanted to help, but instead of words,
flames came out of his mouth, and when
he wished to comfort, he left wounds.
Frightened eyes, fear about nothing,
torn hearts, anything an enemy,
making enemies over nothing.
Agony, and agonizing
about nothing, agitated
about nothing, and not even in pain
despite every pain, and all life
cut up, dissected, and people
misled by pettiness, fleeing
and preening at the same time
since none saw them suffer, and now
this grief about the forsaken,
where nothing has been forsaken,
simply imagined as all well knew,
as no one didn't know, and that's why
hell strikes so many as funny.

EMMA.

What did I see in the dream just now?
It was he who struggled so hard,

and it was me who didn't believe
in him, she who believed in others,
who thought others were in the right
and him in the wrong, who believed him
to be fallen because others
thought so. Why did I turn from him?
Because everyone did and why
did they? That he struggled? Is it not
bright around the strugglers and dark
for the passive? How hard it was
for him. He was covered in rubble.
As soon as he brushed himself off,
new dust fell, but he always got up,
ten, twenty times, if it fell again,
up he'd get again. I found him
once sleeping, his mouth half open,
on the green earth, hands in repose
and delicate like in a portrait,
his chest bare, and above his head
a city, all blue, silver and gold.
O so fragile and beautiful!
And then I saw him without a face
and without limbs, yet I knew him.
How sorry I felt! Suddenly
I saw him alive, limber and strong,
full of passion. 'Ah, he's breaking
his way through now,' I thought, and called him.
He looked around and let me see
his determined face, but already
the flow was pulling him away,

leaving no time. I don't know what
he did, but a voice spoke to me
of joys, festivities, so I
let it be, the way it was.
I believed in this noble man.
I knew that he was good and glad.

THE GOOD-FOR-NOTHING

(1922)

GOOD-FOR-NOTHING. Did I not always tell myself that it will come out fine for me? Even when I ran off, I knew. Isn't that why a fair wind blows? Such is how I love it. That's the way. I needed things in motion around me. I do have the time to reflect now. Nobody has shown up yet, but I hear a harumpher, as if people were here. What a cheerful night! Stars twinkle through the branches. Gold? I need no gold. Silver? I can do without that too. Usually, I don't want to make such aspersions, even less because it seems you gain nothing from it. Have I not won the world? At least I think so myself. I am not rushing you, my friend. A kind of *quantum* of life still stands before you. The twenty years that you reckon still does not count for a stout age. I am still too young to say that I am experienced. How wise I sound! And I come from this journey, standing in this garden now, which I think I recognize. I spent my youth here, performed my first stupid pranks, was in love up to my ears, but it was not just infatuation, it went deeper, otherwise I would not have been drawn back home. A blessed minute which makes me believe that everything is all right now and I must be happy. Why do I think that? Am I gullible? Have I no insight, am I without foresight, without mistrust? Do I have too much trust in myself? Yes, I do, and I hope that is a strength when, if I want to be weak, nothing else will do. A person is the way he is made. As if someone could forbid my eating with my mouth, my putting my hands in my pocket to see if something is there? The pocket is empty. I came home poor. Regardless, I have brought along something: myself. So I am still something. This faith never takes me in. Even now it does not cheat me. Maybe I am not worth it, but why question it? I've hair and teeth, and all kinds of ideas, fingers, feet, and I don't know anything about anything, like others do, and like everybody I feel predestined to marry in the very near future. Marry? What a stupid word! And yet it shimmers on me like the sun, even though it's now night and now only the moon shines down on me. They come! They come! If they ask you anything, answer them with as much wit as possible. In any case, I will not be paying a bit of attention to what I say. I talk about something. Just how is all the same. I have heard the most incredible nonsense said and can swear that the impact and impression, the effect and result were nothing less than intriguing.

CHAMBERMAID. Don't you know me?

GOOD-FOR-NOTHING. Is it possible? Could it be you?

CHAMBERMAID. Who then?

GOOD-FOR-NOTHING. The one, the one I mean.

CHAMBERMAID. You can make up all sorts of things.

GOOD-FOR-NOTHING. Thank God! He who doesn't, doesn't make the right use of his finest virtue. That is not me. As usual, I have been using my imagination and getting by. I was in Italy.

CHAMBERMAID. You?

GOOD-FOR-NOTHING. Of course!

CHAMBERMAID. And where else?

GOOD-FOR-NOTHING. Rome.

CHAMBERMAID. Indeed, that is the capital of that beautiful country. What did you do there?

GOOD-FOR-NOTHING. Not much. I never do much in general. In any case, I never overexert myself. I would never have found that appropriate. Are people not intended to be happy?

CHAMBERMAID. Some say that, but others definitely do not take such a view.

GOOD-FOR-NOTHING. I saw a wonderful water fountain in that splendidly gay moonlight there. Nothing could be more beautiful. O jewel for an hour! You were there, too, even though you will wish to deny it. You looked out the window and gave me a sign. Then—

CHAMBERMAID. Then what?

GOOD-FOR-NOTHING. Someone grabbed me and called me undeservedly a good-for-nothing, bound me up with a deftness which bordered on boldness and blind-folded me as well, with a brazenness which evoked bewitchment. I was lifted into a wagon and carried away.

CHAMBERMAID. Where?

GOOD-FOR-NOTHING. To Venezuela.

CHAMBERMAID. How quickly you lie, and the audacity with which you twist the improbable into the probable borders on magic just as well, like the blindfold around your precious eyes when you wanted to climb through a window. You deserve every rude name possible and, I presume, you could never justify a day in your life.

GOOD-FOR-NOTHING. I dare to doubt that. The gardener in the castle will regret that he called me a lazybones.

CHAMBERMAID. Aren't you?

GOOD-FOR-NOTHING. We should not tell each other the truth, for that leads to the dissolution of fostering conviviality. Am I right or not?

CHAMBERMAID. To some degree I agree with what you say. You know perfectly well how to take advantage of certain principles.

GOOD-FOR-NOTHING. Am I so wrong?

CHAMBERMAID. What happened to you then?

GOOD-FOR-NOTHING. For a time, I lived in a country house there, which was charming. A whimsical madman and a brilliant painter, witches with pointed noses and a dear, dear girl. The breakfast there was renowned. I ate cake whenever I wanted, and in the magnificent garden grew fabulously high trees, defiantly surrounded far and wide by blazing cliffs. I should've stayed there in truth, but I had no residence permit. I thought, too, on and on, about a certain beauty.

CHAMBERMAID. You are probably just pretending to love me?

GOOD-FOR-NOTHING. When it reaches that point, then I'll prove it.

CHAMBERMAID. A wig incomparably high!

GOOD-FOR-NOTHING. That's called confidence. And I wanted to say, that I was in Berlin too.

CHAMBERMAID. When and for how long?

GOOD-FOR-NOTHING. Several years, thus I am a man of the world because who lives in great cities may call himself so.

CHAMBERMAID. But you've never seen the Tyrol?

GOOD-FOR-NOTHING. Well! I've strolled right down the middle and allude to such towns as Meran and Innsbruck. I helped pick juicy grapes there. I can provide you with a postcard from Salzburg with many greetings, which proves I made friends there. I performed there as an actor. What else could I do to get by? For a time I rode on a coachbox as a footman, but, unfortunately, I alienated the gentleman.

CHAMBERMAID. That kind of thing happens. But now?

GOOD-FOR-NOTHING. I take you by the hands and regard you as my wife.

CHAMBERMAID. Ouch, that hurts! Don't squeeze so hard! You're so well-travelled and you have not learned to be more civil? By the way, it's a question of whether I want you, a question of whether you'd make a suitable husband.

COUNTESS. Is that not the gardener's boy, the one who used to sing so pretty?

CHAMBERMAID. The one who put a bouquet of flowers for me every morning on the little garden table?

BAILIFF. The former tax collector?

LEONHARD. The lackey once?

FATHER. That fruitcake of a son?

GOOD-FOR-NOTHING. Do you not know the beautiful city of Vienna with its blue Danube, its glorious woods, the splendid boulevards? Ladies and gentlemen, you may rest assured that I soon mean to move there for a long time. A girl loves me who, indeed, will say the opposite her entire life. But I feel bound to her no matter what. O, if only humourless people prevent her from hearing me! Would it not be best for her, for me? I didn't come into the world as this good little boy. You are patently at fault here, Father dear. Nevertheless, I am grateful. Your bad fruit happily forgives you. From now on, you will see me as a respectable person. For a time, I did think of my ma'mselle here as the Countess. That was naive. But never did I wish it hadn't happened. In fact, I'd love to start all over again from the very beginning, as if it had not happened to me yet. Everybody feels their best in their own clothes. I, however, do take some objection to myself. Now and then I'm content to leave myself open. I listen to a reprimand with pleasure. It's only right, otherwise I worry that it slides off me.

CHAMBERMAID. Are you also this way about praise?

GOOD-FOR-NOTHING. To be honest: No! Praise is a kind of love. Who would want to shake that off? Would it be gallant? Keep your mouth there, and then you will see that I, among other things, have learnt to kiss on my journey, too.

CHAMBERMAID. You'll not unlearn it with me. You'll get plenty of work out of me, and I hope you never get out of the habit of being tender to me. I assume there'll be a steady raise. You must treasure me more day after day, year after year and so win me more and more.

GOOD-FOR-NOTHING. Agreed! Take care that you always stay pretty. And me, I'll take care to remain clever.

CHAMBERMAID. Where did you like it best?

GOOD-FOR-NOTHING. There, where I began, that is, there in the grass as it is so charmingly depicted in our Eichendorff.* In what way did I sense it and feel, for I am hardly this poetic figure or any other? I regarded the flowers there, as they blew back and forth in silent bliss, or, dare I say, rapture amid the gentle breezes, as if they wanted to say in some manner and way: How beautiful and happy we are! I looked into the sky and my head was full of sheer maddening ideas, but I really thought about nothing at all. What should I have studied? I imagined rich, proud cities before me and I believed that I saw them. Later, I really saw them. But those good-for-nothing hours, those of streams rushing, millwheels clattering, of amusing and monosyllabic cluck of the chicken, the chirp of the cricket, the twitter of the swallow, the snap of the teamster's whip and the roll of the wagon are spun together tightly, making life a joy for me. Don't talk. You will not understand. Only a good-for-nothing can. Only he knows what it's like for only he speaks from experience. Doing nothing is a métier as well, it entails many requirements. Sober and industrious people have no idea. How these trees shiver enchantingly with green and light in the hot, yet cool, afternoon. When that arched above me, I closed my eyes and stared blindly into a sea of brilliance, a pair of eyes turned towards me, near and yet inexpressibly far, eyes which resemble yours, you lovely thing—but now nothing more of this bygone time. I declare, once and for all, to overcome all. Strolling has wound down. Points of view are different now. Someone has started to

* Joseph Freiherr von Eichendorff (1788–1857), a German Romantic poet and novelist, famous for his 1826 novella *Aus dem Leben eines Taugenichts* (From the Life of a Good-For-Nothing), which is the inspiration for this dramolette.

place trust in me, so I must, of course, play myself now. It still blows in lightly from the past around a fully occupied mind. What all do I have to do? Appease a bigoted father, kiss a countess' hand, beseech a gardener to change his mind, give a carpenter an order to make furniture because I've built my own house and everything inside should sparkle of newness, furthermore embrace a bride (*he does it*) and laugh from a full throat (*does it*) and be happy, hopefully for ever. Now I'm off to my mother's. She sits in this cosy, quaint little parlour where I once stared lazily outside for days. The woods are nearby, the lovely little garden. She sure will rejoice at my arrival. See how bright it's becoming. Rejoice, clap your hands. Today there should be nobody around who does not agree with himself and his neighbour. Let us decorate our doors and windows with wreathes and then dance together in an open place. Until then, adieu.

PART V

Felix

THE 'FELIX' SCENES

(1925)*

[1]

Felix in front of his parent's shop. He is four or six years old.

FELIX. What all comes to mind and yet I am so small. You could say that I am a pipsqueak. Swallows zip through alleyways and people, so close they practically touch them. All my brothers and sisters already go to school. They do their homework at home, where it is dictated out loud. Given what I know, I know a lot already. That is why others, understandably, have little appreciation for me, and I can see why. How nice it is to be this small. One answers for nothing at all. I am, in many ways, literally still a riddle. All the fine wares in the window. My father's office is at the farthest end of the small alley. I can already guess a little at what the purpose of such an office might be. My sister, who is younger, seems rather demanding. She has this need, from which

* Originally written in 1925 and one of the earliest works Walser composed in the *Mikrogamme* form, that is, in a minute script whose form provides yet another context for the piece. There are illegible words throughout that have been supplied by scholarship and are not indicated in the translation. One of these, however, is the last word, *evergreens* (*Immergrünen*), which is seen as a paean to conformity.

I have already distanced myself, to constantly have a stopper in her mouth, otherwise any situation she finds insufferable makes her cranky. How does one get so dependent? I laugh at her, and when she realizes it, she imparts such a *weepy* expression to her sulking and misery that I am left standing there, taken aback. O how sensitive people are who let themselves be spoilt. I am amazed at my four-year-old eloquence. I would never have taken myself to be this insightful, this smart and circumspect. I literally fascinate myself. How nice it must be to be pleased with myself. I feel that I give some joy to those for whom I feel like being good. The grown-ups provide food. The beds we sleep in are theirs. Feeling the first sparks of knowledge shoot up inside you probably makes life better than possessing the sum of all knowledge, for such a possession must be quite a burden and depressing. My mother is always in a hurry, as if she is unable to devote herself to the many things she would actually rather do. She would spend time with me, if she would let herself. It seems that she is *much* too busy, and here I am practically caring about not having any cares. I long for such cares. When I am grown up, maybe I will not feel the need any more to complain about this shortcoming. How tall the houses are. Now the kids are coming out of the school. It is recess. Butcher, baker and tailor, shoemaker, carpenter, these are tradespeople. I think they call the thing I stand upon the earth. I don't think I matter much to our maid. This sky above me—

MOTHER. What are you doing?

FELIX. Nothing.

[2]

*Outdoor restaurant 'zur Linde'.**

Tables and benches. Fresh green leaves on the hedges.

Flowering cherry trees in the field.

The entire family. It is Sunday.

Felix has drunk the last sip from someone's beer glass.

His outrageous behaviour has been noticed. He gets a beating, which fills him with much needed satisfaction.

One could say it has re-established his equilibrium.

He is delighted with his misbehaviour,
and the spanking has set him straight.

* Ubiquitous name for many hotels and restaurants in German-speaking countries.

[3]

In their father's courtyard, where boxes are stacked,
ADELBERT *and* FELIX.

ADELBERT. What shall we do?

FELIX. I am in the mood for anything.

ADELBERT. Me too.

FELIX. Isn't that Caesar over there?

ADELBERT. Let's make him feel our joined forces. He shall see what it means to stroll carelessly through this back alley. His sunny face offends me.

FELIX. Me too. There is something irritating about the way he walks.

ADELBERT. His unwittingnesses are akin to a challenge.

FELIX. Let's suppose that he is our enemy.

ADELBERT. This gives us reason enough to go after him and all his indiscretion.

FELIX. He thinks about nothing.

ADELBERT. That is outrageous.

FELIX. The simplicity, with which he regards life, gives us the idea that we punish him.

ADELBERT. He deserves to be beaten black and blue, if only for the fact that he is a carpenter's son.

FELIX. I am convinced by your interpretation. But *it* is . . .

They attack CAESAR *and drag him into the courtyard.*

FELIX. Caesar, you are our prisoner. One sound and you will be lying on the ground.

ADELBERT. What fun, to see one of our own kind trembling before us. Your name, little boy.

CAESAR. You know who I am.

FELIX. Do you know who we are?

CAESAR. Why wouldn't I know you?

ADELBERT. What a cocky one, to think he knows us already.

FELIX. He will know us now.

ADELBERT. Beg for mercy.

CAESAR. You should know that once my father hears about this impermissible treatment you are giving me here, he will speak to your father about it.

ADELBERT. He should get one on the head for what he just said.

FELIX. I didn't take him for someone this coldblooded, to be this calm about it.

ADELBERT. He is not as stupid as he likes to appear.

FELIX. Judging by his good attitude, we should make a deal with him.

ADELBERT. So you simply refuse to beg for forgiveness, because of your aimless wandering.

CAESAR. I cannot, not with the best intentions all around me. And I trust you will do nothing indiscreet.

ADELBERT. His running of the mouth deserves praise.

FELIX. If you allow us to slap your face, we will let you go.

CAESAR. I will not accept humiliation of any kind, and I will not consent to even the slightest indignity.

FELIX. Give him a good kick out of the yard.

ADELBERT. I despise him for not letting us despise him.

FELIX. Brilliantly said.

CAESAR. Well, adieu. (*He leaves.*)

ADELBERT. We have let ourselves be influenced by him. Come, let's follow him. Who knows what kind of fun is in store.

MOTHER *opens the window.*

MOTHER. Can't you be quiet? Your brother's really suffering. He is whimpering and all you do is start a fight.

FELIX. All boys feel one and the same about this, that something must be done to have fun. We are healthy and instinctively seek provocation.

MOTHER. Yes, he is sick, and you don't care. Shame on you.

[4]

FELIX *and* FLORI, *his younger sister, standing in front of a house in the New Quarter.*

FLORI. I want to come too. You have to take me along, do you hear, and if you refuse, I will tell Mother and she will punish you. She cannot stand it when I come crying to her, and it pains her. She will take revenge and get back at you. So, you see, you have to obey me.

FELIX. I will not.

FLORI. What? You dare to disagree?

FELIX. I alone have been invited. There was not the slightest mention of you. You have absolutely no tact. You're intrusive. You hang on me.

FLORI. I am making you mad. O, you cannot imagine how this stimulates me. But all that enormous rage of yours, all this projection and prominence to your being annoyed, are in vain. They will not protect you from the idea I so happen to have and points that way. I want you to go inside the house with me for I can see them serving up something good for us to eat.

FELIX. You really have no sense of honour, do you? Don't you see how your hanging on to me is turning me against you?

FLORI. Your frustration is yet another reason to follow you. Even if you don't want me to follow you, you should.

FELIX. I will push you down the stairs.

FLORI. That is just tough talk. You wouldn't dare.

FELIX. I could hit you.

FLORI. You are not mad enough. But Mother must, by all means, be told of your bad behaviour.

FELIX. If I let you come along, will you keep quiet?

FLORI. So, you are afraid of Mother?

FELIX. Not really, just of how she will blame herself afterwards. I feel sorry for her when she gets mad.

FLORI. Your fears seem to be of a different sort than I thought. I shall think about whether to accuse you.

FELIX. If you do accuse me, she will be punished more than me. Don't you feel guilty getting her mad at me when you should be thinking of how she will be hurt for being mad at me?

FLORI. There, if you have such a sensitive disposition, then why do you resist my will?

FELIX *makes a gesture of invitation with his hand. They enter the house,* FLORI *in front with a superior smile on her face.*

[5]

FLORI *and her friend* GRETI *playing with dolls, etc. in the hallway.*

FATHER (*to* FLORI). I just can't see how you can like such a bratty child?

FLORI. Greti is the nicest of all my many, many friends. How heartless you are to me, Father. You will rob me of all my joy. I can see it coming.

FATHER (*in a highly embarrassed voice*). It is very wrong of you to say such a thing. Have I not shown you virtually hundreds of examples of my rather remarkable fondness for you?

FLORI. If you don't think well of Greti, and try to spoil her for me, I will be mad at you.

FATHER (*with laughter he keeps to himself*). I will keep that in mind.

MOTHER (*who has heard everything from the living room*). Are you not ashamed of yourself, to let Flori run circles around you? You really are amazing.

Upon being reproached, FATHER *perhaps makes the most worried face ever made in a family circle. That is, he appears to be extremely worried.*

FELIX. This Greti, with her abundant hair, which frames her not-commonplace face so like a painting. She looks like poetry itself. I can understand Flori. Father's getting kicked around by his baby girl's little slippers, and he shows it a little too overtly, but you have to give him credit. He does deserve something nice.

GRETI. Under Flori's protection, I feel triumphant in this family. My face must be a proud one now. Felix keeps looking at me from a well-calculated distance. I must look really pretty to him. There is nothing more fun than being attractive.

So as not to hurt his daughter FLORI'*s feelings,* FATHER *respects* GRETI. *Although he feels like telling* GRETI *that she does not suit him, but since she does suit his daughter, and because he would not dare hurt her, he makes do with the consolation that* FLORI *and* GRETI *could still have the occasional quarrel. But it does not look that way. They literally seem grafted to each other. The toys are content to be played with by two girlfriends who get along so well. The house, in which such an untouchable girls' friendship thrives, belongs to an upholsterer and is on Madretsch Street.**

FLORI (*to* GRETI). You are welcome over any time.

* A thoroughfare in Biel, Switzerland.

[6]

A neatly furnished, bright room scented, as it were, by bourgeois respectability. Nevertheless, the taste is for the most part provincial. FELIX, *a timid yet unwittingly greedy boy, and his* AUNT, *who, steeped in dignity and bathed by the eleven o'clock morning sun, sits with ladylike dignity in a wingchair quietly happy, as it were, given such a noble burden.*

AUNT. And why have you come? Speak up and for yourself. I don't like this nephewy bashfulness.

FELIX. I shall be as frank as possible just for you and make the following confession. My father sent me.

AUNT. And your mother?

FELIX. No. She talks less and less.

AUNT. Why?

FELIX. Why do you ask? You know why: She is sick.

AUNT. I am sorry to say she has always been very conceited.

FELIX. Aunt, it is a shame you have always been so unkind to her. You have asked me to be frank. This is what results from your request.

AUNT. Continue.

FELIX. My father thought it best to send me to wish you a happy birthday.

AUNT. Tell me, and excuse my interrupting you, what do you think it means to be happy?

FELIX. Health and at most a long, pleasant life.

AUNT. And a fitting vocation.

FELIX. Yes.

AUNT. There is no need to acknowledge what I say. That would be my role. Nodding my head in approval suits me much better.

FELIX. You won't hold my imprudence against me too long.

AUNT. I would think it rather inappropriate. Well?

FELIX. I stand before you, and I hope you will let me say that you have made a relatively good impression on me.

AUNT. Enjoy it.

FELIX. Your furniture is nicer than ours.

AUNT. Do you envy me because of my better furniture?

FELIX. I would not think much of myself if I did that.

AUNT. Your answer pleases me (*gives him a silver thaler* which she takes from her purse with obvious import*). Your father sent you so that I might hand over a silver thaler? Is that not so?

FELIX. Not quite. I believe my father to be a very discreet man.

AUNT. A son should have more deference for his father rather than just talk about him so confidently and complaisantly. And you have not even thanked me that on the occasion of my sixty-fifth birthday I am giving you a present.

FELIX. I hate doing it. I have a virtue called pride.

AUNT. Then let it be. I will assume that you have done it already or will do so in silence. Do I strike you as being a little stern?

FELIX. Because I am comfortable with it, yes. You possess self-esteem. One feels self-assured around you. But I must go now. Someone

* A large silver coin worth about 5 Swiss francs.

is desperately waiting for me downstairs outside the house. Someone whose company is so dear to me that I regret every minute I cannot spend with him.

AUNT. Where? What?

FELIX. Being in his company.

AUNT. It has to be a friend. (*She remains seated and* FELIX, *who dashes off, bids her farewell.*)

[7]

In front of a stationer's shop. HANS *is staring into the shop window.*

FELIX (*looks him over, a few steps away*). I must be careful with my urge to make an overture to him. I have liked him to myself for a while now. He might notice. How that would make him strong. Just the idea of it turns me into my own teacher who reproaches me with an angry face. How he stands there in contemplation, as if staring at himself in a mirror. Why does he seem so handsome to me? Because he is vain? Is he? He does not have any friends, nobody likes him, and he doesn't even seem to notice. Does he like himself, and is that enough for him? Does he think so much of himself that he is satisfied with his own friendship? How harmlessly he turns his back to me. How his examination becomes him. Only someone spoiled could stay this calm. His composure upsets me. Seeing him in such self-rapport makes me angry with myself. In no way does he seem lonely, even though he is. Why does he seem both so tender and at the same time so self-possessed, and why doesn't he wonder what is happening next to him and behind him? There is something of a good upbringing about him, but it is probably much more. It is innate. So he has no need to be more curious than to coexist with beauty. Perhaps he has few qualities, perhaps only one, but one makes him rich. I sink into poverty at the mere sight of this richness and thus better pull myself away. I would rather not speak to him. It would sound too polite, and then he would smile, and I am not willing to grant him this good fortune, even if I would be terribly happy to give him a reason to be happy. Knowing, how wicked you are. (*He leaves.*)

HANS (*in error*). Go to them, to those who are strangers to me.

[8]

During religion class.

THE PASTOR. Before I leave you today, I must inform you that our fatherland is being threatened by an unforeseen incident. A citizen of a neighbouring kingdom has behaved in an unseemly manner on our soil, and, as a result, has been confronted and consequently expelled from our country. With the force of indignation, the leading man of our neighbouring realm, a highly reputable statesman, has addressed our highest officeholder, seeking an apology, which is something that cannot remain unanswered for every country's representatives must retain their influence, which is to say that they protect our interests. This should be plain to you. There are increasingly outspoken voices that have even reached us, that speak of the most unpleasant prospect that peaceful people could imagine. May God in his mercy protect our little country from the outbreak of war. With that, our lesson is over.

The pupils shudder at the profound, faceless danger staring at them.
It is the veiled faces of the Furies. They whisper.
This time the classroom does not empty with the usual speed.
It occurs to them that all the historical events their teachers have talked about in class could come true. They all feel strange.
Nobody says a word. They are stunned, bewildered.

[9]

The chalet of FRAU ZIERLICH. *She is, incidentally, a canton counsellor. Is that important? We are afraid that in these days this no longer has an awe-inspiring effect.*

FELIX *and* HEINRICH, *the counsellor's son, are eating pastries.*

FRAU ZIERLICH (*appears in the front door*). So you are friends again. Let's hope you don't fight again anytime soon.

FELIX. I am almost sorry about this armistice despite my being happy about it. I think I already feel a little bored. There is nothing more exciting than war.

FRAU ZIERLICH. What caused you to fight him, to rouse the entire classroom against him?

FELIX. Before I tell you, I must suppress my laughter.

FRAU ZIERLICH. You should follow the example of today's nice weather and try being polite.

FELIX. Many, many apologies.

FRAU ZIERLICH. One would do.

FELIX. So I started hating Heinrich because he wears such outrageously high-top shoes and because his pants fit him so well.

FRAU ZIERLICH. You are offended by his fine appearance?

FELIX. I find him to be a bit of a mamma's boy.

FRAU ZIERLICH. And you dare tell me that, his mother?

FELIX. And he was always in much too good of a mood. His perpetual cheerfulness stirred rebellious thoughts in me. And I was overcome with this wish, this desire to make his life miserable. He trusted me too much. He thought he was, just like that, my dearest friend. In a way he was. I could even swear by it. But because he was, he could no longer be my friend. Facts exist primarily to be denied. Reality seems a little intrusive.

FRAU ZIERLICH. I ask you, in all seriousness, not to turn Heinrich here into the object of your impudence. Unfortunately, you seem a bit too spirited. But you should know that our spirits have to be tamed. Please take it easy in the future, will you?

FELIX. Perhaps with more pastries.

FRAU ZIERLICH. In the interest of such a pleasant day, which seems to guarantee this new friendship between you and Heinrich, I am more than happy to meet your terms, though I find them pert. (*Enters the house.*)

HEINRICH. I think Mama respects you.

FELIX. She should indeed need such regard for one so compliant.

HEINRICH. Can I trust you now?

FELIX. You have to take your chances. But you should always mistrust me a little.

HEINRICH. Flattering yourself?

FELIX. Come, let's walk across the meadow. It will be splendid when your mother sees we found it inconvenient to be waiting for the delivery of our request. One must always show that one can do without kindness and good will. Let's build a clubhouse?

HEINRICH. Good, let's do that.

[10]

FELIX (*in a tree*). Climb up too. It is wonderful up here. You cannot imagine how lofty it feels. Now I can understand the freebooters, those American buccaneers in stories told to me. I feel like I am in jungle-bush country. The souls of Barbary Pirates—wait, let me first reflect before I continue with my fire tale on high. Introductions are always bold, but every beginning requires the contemplation of its instalments. Lord Byron, Mazepa.* How meekly and yet almost impetuously I envy the adventures this Pole lived. To find yourself surrounded by Cossacks, half dead, with a snow-white body glistening, peppered with wounds, and bandaged and adored by a Hetman's daughter. What a delightful way to go. Her mercy, his feverish fantasies, and the hut, in which he lies still, the bed and the vast yellow steppe, the faces looking on and the tea, or whatever it might be he is sipping, and the whispering: 'He sleeps,' the warm respect of these strange, earthy people, the all-hearing ears, that sleeping with their eyes open, the thinking without thought. Please try. All pretty and eventful tales flutter about me like little buntings. I am like an Indian who lives, kissed by this breeze, in the highest room of a seven-hundred-room palace. You can hear me dream, hear me happy. I hear the sea. I am the keen captain of a gay flying ship. My sailors, with their devotion and lightning-fast discharge of their duty, leave nothing to be desired. The coral bays smile at me from a blue-hazed distance like strangely beautiful

* George Gordon Byron (1788–1824), English Romantic poet; the allusion is to his service as a volunteer in the cause of Greek independence; Ivan Stepanovych Mazepa (1639–1709), the Cossack Hetman and an important figure in Russian and Ukrainian history.

women, and you still have little or no desire at all to climb up here and be friend and companion to my subtly fragrant and exceedingly agreeable circumstances. O how I, up here, pity you down there, branch-like and twig fine. If it now were night and an enchantress turned me into a glittering, silver-hammering, zigzag-singing nightingale swooping from one aural ecstasy to another, and children listening to me from their rooms, where they have perhaps already snuggled into their cots, where they have said their prayers perhaps. From here I peer into a chapel hall, and there at the window, just a short way away. A lady now appears wearing an embroidered, lovingly pleated morning robe, in a house that seems to be her own for she looks very much the homeowner. A certain originality shows from her every subdued motion, and all neighbouring trees wish that I had honoured every single one of them with my blithe and unexpected visit.

THE WOMAN WHO OWNS THE TREE. What, to my horror, must I be looking at?

RUDOLF. Now you've done it.

THE FRIGHTENED WOMAN. O, my poor trees. Stay there. I want to blame this on you with your poor, suffering parents present.

FELIX. Why poor?

THE WOMAN. Because they call such a scamp as you their own.

FELIX. I request a somewhat more conciliatory title, if I may. I command a frigate. Can't you see that I am an Indian chief?

The WOMAN, *who doesn't want to understand, shrilly orders him to climb down from his ascended height and the stateroom of a commodore to the reality of Central Street.*

[11]

FELIX *in bed, with a burnt face.*

THE DOCTOR. How did this happen?

FELIX. Me and him . . .

THE DOCTOR. Who is 'him'?

FELIX. Hegi.

THE DOCTOR. When someone asks you for an accurate account, you must provide one.

FELIX. Hegi and I had a squib.

THE DOCTOR. What does that mean? Express yourself in layman's terms and not so expertly.

FELIX. A squib means a firework. We wanted to light one of these.

THE DOCTOR. You simply wanted to?

FELIX. At first we just wanted to. For a time we only toyed with the idea. Then we carried it out step-by-step. Then came the execution and the entire charge blew up in my face. Unfortunately, I put my hands to my injured face.

THE DOCTOR. You shouldn't have done that.

FELIX. It happened, nevertheless.

THE DOCTOR. So it has, consequently.

FELIX. Without the shadow of a doubt. My face is irrefutable evidence. I am proud of the adventure.

THE DOCTOR. Which could have cost you your eyesight.

FELIX. So it went well.

THE DOCTOR. You should rest now. That is the price for playing with fire.

FELIX. For the first time in my life, even though it is yet a young and inconsequential life, I am sick in bed. For me, there is something charming about that. I cannot express it any other way.

THE DOCTOR. You obviously feel quite honoured by my visit.

FELIX. Yes, there is something genteel about being sick. They handle you with respect, look at you thoughtfully. One sick is the object of increased attentiveness. This can only flatter one.

THE DOCTOR. As long as you find such sunny words, it is not a serious illness, and there is nothing serious to worry about. But you should not flatter yourself so much.

FELIX. I just wanted something to say as well.

THE DOCTOR. In eight days you will be cured.

[12]

FELIX *is helping his* MOTHER *in the kitchen.*

FELIX (*in the mood for Swiss history*). So they had already achieved much success in all directions, which perhaps resulted now and then in their becoming overconfident. It was during the fifteenth century, and I regret that I was unable to personally experience the draperies and colours of this stirring epoch.

MOTHER. You think of yourself as a heroic figure.

FELIX. One can easily imagine something beautiful and great and need not be hindered by washing dishes. That is precisely why we live in a finer, softer time. Our obligations are of a different kind. Now, when they reached the summit of their fame, which they achieved with apparently honest devices, which strained all their blithesomeness about life, so to speak, soon enemies appeared, first here, then there, in such superior numbers that they would have been—given enough time—shocked. It once so happened they were surrounded, utterly bated, but strangely enough undefeated, that is, they were defeated and still victors nonetheless, which maybe is the best way to leave a mighty impression in your enemy's chest. Soon after they assessed the price of being extraordinarily brave and rose, with the help of the most prudent leadership imaginable, to a kind of peak of power, from which skill is entailed to get down from, which in turn led them to realize their lack of the necessary tools and equipment, that which the relegators of their glory were copiously supplied in. So, dressed in their wounds and furnished with the diplomas of their tragic effort, they descended from the high hills, yes indeed one could say mountains of their medals, with slow, cautious steps, down to the plains of their apparently appropriate place and settled for the preservation of their kind and with their sincerely hard-fought and otherwise self-imposed humility.

MOTHER. Listening to your words has made me burn the noodles.

FELIX. There will be some faces made at lunch.

MOTHER. It might be better if you loved your history a little less.

FELIX. But it is so glorious. When I get involved in history, with all of its exemplary figures, I feel so happy to be alive.

MOTHER. One can be too healthy, feel too robust sometimes.

FELIX. One submits to his talents involuntarily and instinctively.

MOTHER. You always know better than your mother, unfortunately. One day you will suffer for it.

FELIX. Do you wish that on me?

MOTHER. You are a little boy of luxury. Your kind are made to perturb.

FELIX. Whatever, all the more entertaining.

MOTHER. You always think about your books, but never about me. One day there will be many people complaining to you about your wealth of concerns. They will scold you. They will point at you and say: See, the one with no soul!

FELIX. When one is apathetic to nothing, it looks like one is apathetic to everything.

MOTHER. It is a real shame about these noodles. I am worried now.

FELIX. How this sensitive person suffers from this little mistake. Everything comes down to whether we feel it or not. (*Loudly*) I am to blame for this. You can tell them that.

MOTHER. This observation pleases me. I feel calmer now.

[13]

FELIX appears, barefoot, that is, without shoes and socks, in the 'nice room'. This is, as it were, how a parlour is described in a small town, what one would call a 'salon' in the capital.

OLDER BROTHER. Can't you be a little more careful?

FELIX. What do you mean?

OLDER BROTHER. I am not happy with your total arrogance, as you would seem to expect from me. Since when does one act so informally at home? An older brother should not be treated with absolutely no respect by the younger. I should not have to remind you of that. You should know better.

FELIX. In principle, you are right.

OLDER BROTHER. And then you clearly wanted to make me mad, perhaps out of boredom, and because you know of my regard for form. Admittedly, even if I am too punctilious, I would like to remind you, nevertheless, of the necessity to behave properly, to at least try.

FELIX. I thought it stood out presenting myself with naked feet for you this one time. It has something of the beggar boy about it, something Neapolitan.

OLDER BROTHER. I am incapable of lending dignity to bad manners.

FELIX gets upset because he upset his OLDER BROTHER and withdraws cautiously. The battlefield is being maintained by someone who would rather he not bother making such demonstrations. Often a victor must battle much harder with himself than the one who has been driven off.

[14]

ADELBERT *in the kitchen.* FELIX, *hesitating, enters.*

FELIX. What it costs me, this hesitant step forwards towards conquest in my proud, brotherly soul, you are hardly resolved to esteem. Your face in no way shows the necessary energy to appreciate me finger-thick or -long and what I am setting out to do here, for this kitchen shall witness one of the boldest, most fearless and probably most audacious acts ever attempted by anyone. I speak in digressions so as to run circles around the hot porridge,* as it is almost the proper thing to do. The way you watch me, dull and impertinent, but the face you make is not real, it is insincere, and it well may be that you shiver, like you do before me now, this new arrival, this pretending to be cold adverse or poised for any situation. No, you have not been poised, such that I would interrogate you now, and so you make a real face, as if you were not surprised, but that way you are likewise satisfied from being surprised. Watch me with your eyes wide open and seemingly self-composed. You are not self-composed, for you are overjoyed at my arrival, I know how overjoyed you are now, even though I know quite well that you will reject such an assessment of yourself. We passed each other by for two long months without making any attempt to acknowledge the other, and we would have had we not made ourselves enemies. But if you think that this separation was absolutely unendurable to me, you are making a very big mistake. I would have put up with our unfriendliness for as long as you, and you will never succeed in making me think that you suffered almost as much as me. This very minute

* From the German idiom expressed 'to run like a cat around the hot porridge'; cf. to 'beat around the bush'.

you suffer more than me, for you stand there incredibly antagonistic, and this splendid show of defiance is simply nothing more than a miserable lie whose scope is now out in the open. And when you give me your face with such unbelievably incredible pains, wanting to drape contempt around my action, which wraps me in such malevolence, you fight the much-too-hard fight with your breast, which is full of ebullient friendship for me, which you have just grown accustomed to, forbid yourself. I tremble, and don't you really tremble too? Must the unforgiven not tremble before those who forgive them? Of course, I did not come here, where you, for whatever reasons, just now looked into the breadbox, in order to forgive you, which would not be the right approach. I rather came here in all seriousness to beg for your forgiveness, which I am sure you have already granted me in spirit since you have been longing for some natural contact with me. Indeed, I myself am aware of how someone begging for peace can only feel degraded, albeit I did not feel degraded, but rather with heart high, lit by something like an Alpine magnificence of feeling inside, and it must shine inside you as well, and because of me you owe me this beauty even though I see and feel how difficult it is for you to open your closed mouth just ever so slightly. I feel as if I have not seen you for a long time, as if you have disappeared for a while, as if I saw you for the first time after this long period of lost existence to me. And yet we still looked at each other every day, but how? Certainly not because it made us happy.

ADELBERT. Today, I am happy to see you.

FELIX. At last.

ADELBERT. What?

FELIX. Words.

ADELBERT. Words that have cost me so much renunciation from my half-fond grudge, as you will hardly ever understand.

FELIX. But I do.

ADELBERT. Please let me be for a while.

FELIX. Fine.

ADELBERT. I might be able to see you and your ways in the right light.

FELIX. We have made our peace, and you wish to rejoice in silence for a while.

ADELBERT. What I still don't quite concede to you . . .

FELIX. What? There is still something you don't concede to me?

ADELBERT. . . . is that you found such courage steeped in love. I would never have thought you so big-hearted.

FELIX. You honour me because you are happy. (*He leaves.*)

ADELBERT. Why have I requested more time to consider it? Do I have something to consider? (*He calls.*) Felix!

FELIX. So you are willing to welcome me into the living-room of your reborn or, perhaps in part, even fresh outburst of affection?

ADELBERT. I must say it was boring to be your foe.

FELIX. And that means respect is more cordial than disrespect.

ADELBERT. We will now speak of it no more.

[15]

FELIX *and* A STUDENT FROM BERN, *who is on holiday, standing upon a high place. Romantic rocks, oak trees.*

THE STUDENT FROM BERN. This Shakespeare, whose name sounds so strange to us, was born in Stratford-upon-Avon.

FELIX. I already read that somewhere, someplace.

THE STUDENT. They say he was a clerk at first and worked for a lawyer, after which he moved to London to make his living composing plays, which for him was successful. It is said he set himself up as a landlord. He also performed in his own plays as an actor. Legend has it he got himself into trouble and was arrested on stage, in front of a full house. The queen was there, surrounded by her ladies and cavaliers, and as a sign of her approval, she tossed a bouquet for the poet and actor, most likely when the bailiffs appeared to arrest the author before everyone's eyes, undone only by the monarch's wink. Shakespeare came to the front of the stage, bent a knee for his protectress and played on confident and carefree.

FELIX. How many plays did he write?

THE STUDENT. Around thirty or forty, I cannot give you an exact number. In any case, he produced an amazing body of work. In the literary field, he was a potent sire, seldom seen. And his numerous children are still alive, ever to be performed by us with passion and success as well.

FELIX. Are they really so good that we have the courage to perform them over and over again?

THE STUDENT. They are full of authentic characters. Take Julius Caesar, for example. We cannot see him in any other way than he has been shown for us. A prince has his eyes gouged out. A father, although betrayed by two of his daughters, their being bored, calls them virtuous and good. The third, whom he misunderstands and rejects, keeps worshipping him on high and must die for the sake of this emotive beauty, and then he, with this impoverished failure at self-recognition, embraces her corpse in the madness that overcomes him because his reason can no longer endure his suffering.

FELIX. How beautiful and how terrible.

THE STUDENT. Art meant that the entire gravity of human nature have a mellowed taste and echoed by beautiful melodies, and that we be reconciled to evil when it shows itself in all its permutations. Shakespeare produced countless, highly eccentric villains. He even created a jealous one who took care in being perfectly thorough in bringing off the stabbing death of his wife in bed.

FELIX. Such a thing must work like magic on stage.

THE STUDENT. It does. A general, who nourishes grand ideas, pits himself against one of the highest figures in the kingdom and falls, and his fall is something monumental. A pair of siblings finds each other again in the most fairy-tale way, and then he sprinkles every work with so many supporting characters, as many as a curious, entertainment-starved audience could want. If you arranged them one after the other, you would get a long, long procession full of the most colourful costumes, like a rich band, a sash.

FELIX. It is such a pleasure to listen to you. One gets the impression you are from Bern, from circles thirsty for knowledge.

THE STUDENT. To have such an appreciative, I would almost say, rapt listener makes this conversation a pleasure.

FELIX. Then we both please the other.

THE STUDENT. Indeed, and this is how it could always be, wherever there are people with the right attitude. It all depends on a healthy attitude.

FELIX. You did me a service, and one for yourself.

THE STUDENT. I was inspired and passed on that inspiration to you.

FELIX. O, if we could just always find inspirational subjects. How much we owe the greats who dared what is pleasing and complex.

THE STUDENT. Shall we still practise some gymnastics?

[16]

A letter from THE STUDENT *to* FELIX.

When I came to visit my family, you let me have a look inside your attic room as well as at your honest love spent on books. That is why I still do not see a future of bookworminess in you by any length. We both waded deeply through extensive and pleasant conversations. I will always remember their tenor. In addition to my studies, I occasionally practice the high bar, the one found in the garden which belongs to the house in which I currently reside. Be so kind as to delight me with a visit of yours sometime. The train fare is not that expensive. Try to watch your pocket money (*reading this sentence,* FELIX *thought of the* Collected Works of Voltaire). The classics, which you have amassed, have not only been purchased by you, but also read by you. Reading is certainly not as wasteful as some people make it out to be, and do not let yourself be intimidated by your Papa. There is no doubt he means well, and when he suggests that you should no longer care for intellectual pursuits, it is your duty to understand him, thus you never need follow his advice. His benevolence makes him fear all sorts of possibilities, like his sons not being prosperous enough. He sees this dwelling on beautiful literature as a mere diversion, as one of many things that distract from the appropriate, while it is simply education and not dissipation. I enjoyed your fine garretical joys, and when you find the time and need to step up to the desk which I left behind for your use, write me a letter. I promise that I will welcome your every written expression. I find the pavilion's view of the lake as magnificent as you likely do. Always be at once affectionate and prudent, and do not think that I say this only to you. He who expresses something that is right, or something that at least seems important to him, above all rights himself as well. You and I are now of an age when patience sometimes turns into torture. With best wishes.

[17]

FELIX *in the attic.*

FELIX (*in conversation with the* Collected Works of Voltaire). Beyond doubt you have wit, yet the genteel language you employ, the great thoughts on which you leave your imprint, will leave me cold. Only to the apathetic will I praise all your superior virtues. I hope that you will allow for it. You see, I have no spending money, but would love to have some, and you just lie there so alone, so neglected, so altogether unopened. You should be of service to something, you. How many volumes do you amount to? One volume the same as the next. It looks like a column of soldiers. I am convinced you are worth reading, yet I am even more convinced that I would prefer carrying you to the antiquarian bookseller on Untergasse* and sell you. I sincerely ask that you forgive my lack of culture, for which I am guilty. I shall take you under my arm, in all of your collectivity and completeness, and slip out of the house. Mother is having tea with Miss Pflüger, the governess who has lived many an adventure in Romania, and Father is busy walking the city streets. It is a good opportunity, the time is right. I want to take advantage of this overly gilded, convenient opportunity, which might not show itself again for quite some time. (*He leaves with his merchandise.*)

* A street in Biel, known for its second-hand and antique dealers (*Althändler*).

[18]

At the family's midday meal. The new PROFESSOR.

PROFESSOR. You should be pleased with such healthy offspring.

FATHER. But until every child has learned something, the studies of these two here, you know very well how much that costs. Please help yourself. That's why the food is here.

MOTHER. But Father, you are pressuring the Professor as if he were some local. You are forgetting how to be proper.

PROFESSOR. It is exceedingly kind of your husband.

ARNOLD. Material interests are, if need be, subordinate to the so-called good of intellectual interests.

FATHER. So called? Allow me to tell you . . .

PROFESSOR. I am convinced your son will go far in the academic world. His current views are already of desirable depth.

FATHER. The roast veal most sincerely wishes to be enjoyed.

MOTHER. How you always go on about the food. You must think others share your interest.

PROFESSOR. I admire your husband, and I have no doubt the sacrifices he is making for his sons now will be appreciated and worthwhile.

FATHER. The worries.

MOTHER. Don't speak of your worries in the presence of this gentleman. You are embarrassing yourself.

PROFESSOR. Please allow your dear husband to embarrass himself a little in my humble presence. It is indeed no small thing to be facing financial difficulties.

ARNOLD. There is a viewpoint from which the subjugation of a minor hardship ought not to be rated so highly as it seems one should.

FATHER. So, a minor hardship? Allow me to observe . . .

MOTHER It would be appropriate for you to remain silent.

ARNOLD. You just have it with everyone today.

MOTHER (*fuming*). Yes! (*With full and therefore almost beautiful force, she throws a knife against the wall above the* PROFESSOR'S *head.*)

FATHER. Why are you so upset again? You really shouldn't be.

MOTHER What?

PROFESSOR. All of you are, I must admit, highly interesting. (*He laughs.*)

ARNOLD. My mother's behaviour is caused by a nervous condition.

MOTHER. Caused by what, you brat.

ARNOLD. You must excuse us, Professor.

MOTHER. Heartless son.

PROFESSOR. O, he is certainly not that yet. The family, in whose circle I have the honour to be sitting, is in my view simply going through a difficult time.

MOTHER. Of course, you are here to help, and I should have realized that.

PROFESSOR. Please forgive me if I have displeased you.

FATHER. You see?

MOTHER. Yes, you can immediately see his experience. If only you had as much experience.

PROFESSOR. I am sorry to see how you do enjoy underestimating your husband just slightly.

MOTHER. Because of his well-directed speech, so I hope you will not blame me. (*She offers her hand to her husband.*)

ARNOLD. There will be times . . .

MOTHER. Enough about the times.

PROFESSOR. And what would you like to be?

FELIX. Thank God I am in the most perfect indecision about that.

PROFESSOR. Your answer should cause some concern. I prefer, however, to see you as a strong young person.

FELIX. One doesn't need to be very useful.

MOTHER. The way you speak.

PROFESSOR. He may not be speaking so foolishly. He shows intellect.

FATHER. Unfortunately all he does with his free time is read books.

FELIX. Father means well. (*He thinks about the student's letter.*)

MOTHER. We have certainly been quite worried that you might leave here without a good impression of us.

PROFESSOR. Your worry flatters me. You are a good soul.

ARNOLD. Your kindness . . .

MOTHER. Don't you dare come at me with your critique of kindness.

PROFESSOR. Your mother is certainly jealous of your knowledge, your intelligence to which you apply yourself, and I hope I have paid her a compliment by saying so.

MOTHER. Once you have left us, your devoted servant will miss something.

ARNOLD. Don't be so subservient. You're embarrassing me.

FATHER. It would do you little if any harm if your mother embarrasses you now and then.

ARNOLD *attempts to rise from the table.*

MOTHER. Just remain seated. I am afraid I am unable to present you with my eldest daughter because we could not find her. She is someplace where she likes it better than here at home.

PROFESSOR. O, I am sure you are doing her an injustice. You are sensitive.

MOTHER. It is a pity I am.

FATHER. Cheer up.

MOTHER. Seems as though one must with such a cheerless husband.

PROFESSOR. Don't be resentful. You have the most well-bred children.

MOTHER. And the most ill-bred mother is asking, as a sign that this meal is now over, for permission to leave the table. I am sure it would give us great pleasure if you stayed for a while longer. I will now serve coffee in the parlour.

They rise from the table.

[19]

MOTHER *writes to her eldest daughter, who works as a hotel switchboard operator.* FELIX *watches her. One should think of her handwriting as at once crabbed, yet slightly florid. A curious blend of the salon and folk.*

Dear Daughter, I don't know if I have given it enough thought before I put pen to paper, that said, you know how it really bothers me knowing that you are very far away from me in surely very elegant and comfortable circumstances which, perhaps, are too comfortable for you, too entertaining, such that you have all but forgotten about me already since it seems I rarely get news from you. The tables laid, the halls, the shiny waxed floors and the musicians, which cater to the flattery of the senses, are already causing you to neglect what the Bible tells us and how its words warn us against temptation. Having you up there, where the international rich saunter about and idleness looks for diversion and makes advances with such skill, fills me with worry, and I would remind you (*she hesitates, as if she were in doubt, as if she were fighting with truth*) of chastity, of those who should remember to be virtuous, who should always want to comply no matter what. You are pretty, and you will enjoy every time they make you feel so in a nice way, but I am no longer pretty, and do you really want to have it on your conscience for my being left so alone, for I am alone despite having a husband, him who feels not what I feel. Please come home.

She cries. FELIX *quickly leaves the room, so that she does not notice that he was watching her. One often sends letters simply to ensure that their content no longer afflicts us. Perhaps that was the case here as well.*

[20]

In a courtyard where old scraps of iron, etc., lie about.

FELIX (*to a caged owl*). How can you be so silent, even you? Don't you call this overdoing the aloofness? Perhaps you are more important than you seem? Say something. So you have no desire to share something. Are you sleeping, Fraulein? This face that never changes surely won't do. This is not a mime show. You really have nothing to say to me, Amalie? This is the park, and Karl has at present plenty to do in the Bohemian woods. So, in this case, my name is Franz, and I would like to ask you for a small sign of your affection. Do you consider your forlornness an expression of speech enough? I can see myself losing my patience with you. How long have you been sitting here like this? Tell me, please tell me. O, speak! Do you call not one syllable of response talking, and do I have to figure on future incomprehensibilities given your boding the monotonous display? Are you a deception, or are you as you seem? No answer for such a franzical question? The Old Moor is installed in the tower.* How can you stare so unmoved? O your round eyes seem to hold all the world's wisdom. Did you know that I am leaving school in eight days to begin my apprenticeship? And are you aware how great Shakespeare is? And do you want to spend the rest of your life in this wire cage? But perhaps there is a point to this pointlessness. Does your dream of love, your dream of loyalty, cause you to feel nothing for these passing, fading moments? Don't you ever, ever find it sad around you, around one such a beauty?

* The speech alludes to characters in Friedrich von Schiller's play *Die Räuber* (*The Robbers*, 1781): Maximilian, Count von Moor (the 'Old Moor'), his two rival sons, Karl and Franz.

What did you do to lose your song-singing, bliss-mirroring throat, such that your neck merged with your head, as though any fine line were forever superfluous? Was it your homesickness for Karl's heart that made you so ugly? Away, Franz, it does seem she wants to remain silent. What shall I do with this enigmatic lady? She might think she talks. Perhaps she does, but I can't hear any of it. And now another comes toward me to suffer me. Owls, owls everywhere. The ancient miracles are among us still. Where I imagine myself to be, there might be a Kyrgyzstan. Thus, is not almost anything possible? I step backwards, but really I am marching forwards. There is great improvidence in all assertions. Some of my friends no longer know me because the other sphere is already visible in my face. Pass your time, my little treasure. There is not one person alive who can do you any good. O, if I turned into an owl and nothing would move me, nothing would interest me. Is that not celestially thought? I must flee, or she will bewitch me. I do not like to be reminded so precociously of ambiguity.

[21]

In FELIX's FATHER's *small office. This concerns a minor, honest broker, who seemingly has no character at all, regrettably doing nothing but answer to miserable hardship. The not-well-to-do cannot be this thing we call character. It is up to the well-to-do to embellish the position that they occupy with this trinket.*

FATHER. Listen for once.

FELIX. I'm listening.

FATHER. Your superior is such a charming man.

FELIX. Father dear, perhaps he only seems that way to you.

FATHER. Treating your objection with due disregard, something you will understand, let me tell you with all paternal friendship, which I kindly request you trust in, that your chief complains of your deportment, he tells me that you refuse to talk to him, that you never speak. And yet he is satisfied with you. In fact, he praised your diligence and intelligence. What do you have to say for yourself?

FELIX. Your sympathetic consent of my principal's sensitivities amazes me, with your permission, of course, for there is no other way that I can explain his accusation against me. Is it not the job of the boss to speak rather than the apprentice? Why, if it appears he is ready to confer with me, doesn't he convene a conference, him, the dominant one? I am under him, he is over me. He is the powerful one, I am the weak one. I find it funny that behind my back he is defending himself from his assistant, he, the teacher, against his student. He just holds something against me. It would look better, be more robust and befitting his position if he knew how to deal with it or drop it. The high ones should first and foremost be the ones who are open, inspire confidence, or no? If I dare speak to him in confidence, he should feel free to tell me to my face that I am rude. His seat, on which he sits, empowered him not to have much ado with me.

FATHER. So this is how you speak of your director?

FELIX. Who makes detours around me.

FATHER. Who is thought to be such a charming man.

FELIX. People will say such things the day blue.

FATHER. I am worried about you, son.

FELIX. Father, you give me cause for concern.

FATHER. Concern doesn't suit you. It is better we end this discussion. Life, it seems, will have to teach you some important lessons.

FELIX. I hope for much from my girlfriends, those experiences I have yet to know.

FATHER. I am sure they will reveal themselves to you. You are free to go.

FELIX. Everywhere you look is hardship, inadequacy, half-smiling and half-grim.

FATHER. You can mail this letter for me since I have your nimbleness at my disposal. (*He hands him the mail.*)

[22]

FELIX's *letter to Ernst Possart, you know, the actor.**

Great and true Master, I beg you, despite the laurels that hang inside your vast apartments, to read this letter from a small-town boy who saw illustrated magazine pictures of you and whose only glowing wish is to ascend the heights of the theatrical world if to climb is not quite the right expression. I read Schiller and Goethe, and my dwelling, with your permission, is a bare-walled attic room with a small window through which I often stare in your direction. I have written a letter to a local artist friend of mine, who lives in a fabulously beautiful snow-white, garden-enclosed villa, in regard to my plans for the theatre. He has, however, to my immeasurable regret, advised against my intentions. Perhaps you, for want of time to bother with one's dream-invented career, will do the same too. I can only guess that many, many young folk contemplating the stage write you, and it is not very hard to see that it is impossible for you to send for every young person for a proper dramatic education, which is undoubtedly an exercise in patience. O smile and at least answer me from your artistic heights. You can hardly imagine the positive joy a short note from you would give me. My father has no idea, not even an inkling that I long for the stage with every fibre of my being, about which I have the most auspicious designs, for I see it as a noble, far-reaching institution, full of expeditiousness and virtual devotion. Actually, I am very surprised at the courage I found in myself to turn to such a famous personality, and in this spirit, I bow to you.

* Ernst Possart (1841–1921), German actor and theatre director.

[23]

A mountainside in spring. FELIX'*s apprenticeship has long been over. He keeps, as we will presently hear, sensitive women company.*

FELIX. It is sweet with violets. Smell them?

FRAU ELEONORE. Does he write you?

FELIX. I can well guess of whom you speak, but for now may I ask you of whom do you speak?

ELEONORE. Of him who thinks highly of you.

FELIX. Actually, Jacob has, whether unconsciously or by design, a rather low opinion of you.

ELEONORE. After such words I should really ask you to leave.

FELIX. But you wanted to know if he writes me?

ELEONORE. I know he does. By the way, I am amazed at the meticulous way you dress these days.

FELIX. Do you respect me for it?

ELEONORE. You should know us women.

FELIX. The city below us has something of a mistress about it. I might add that it reminds me of responsibilities and foretells that it could please.

ELEONORE. How calculated you talk. Do you do this to hurt me?

FELIX. How sensitive you are. Is it because you love him but don't get love in return?

ELEONORE. Are your inconsiderate words because it is spring, which reminds us of all that is tender?

FELIX. I speak this way to elicit your reply. He holds me in high esteem and you don't get this.

ELEONORE. The city below reminds me of many sleepless nights.

FELIX. It must be very monotonous to lie in bed without being able to sleep. I would see unrequited love as monotonous. I would rather have any kind of work than sentimental futility.

ELEONORE. Go fetch me those primroses looking at me so friendly like.

FELIX. They only seem to be looking at you. Otherwise leave this phrase in a book. Flowers do not sprout so as to have eyes for us people. They are blind and holy. Whenever I see such a small flower, everything that is pointless about our existence stands in the way of my capacity to apprehend, and I do not want to pick it. I am not your lackey.

ELEONORE. Snake.

FELIX. Me?

ELEONORE. Yes.

FELIX. The flowers of spring do not smile the way we do. To me they are too beautiful, too important for mere petulance. You could just as well ask me to pick that horse there, I want to take it home with me.

ELEONORE. Do you despise me?

FELIX. Absolutely.

ELEONORE. You won't be able to explain it to me.

FELIX. Why not?

ELEONORE. You don't feel anything for women.

FELIX. Why don't I?

ELEONORE. Because you are so boorish.

FELIX. Why am I boorish? All I do is stand up for myself. A woman who dares speak to a man of her impulsivities not only fails to respect herself, but her companion too to the degree she should.

ELEONORE. You are more kind-hearted than you pretend to be.

FELIX. I would treat a girl with tenderness who speaks to me of immaterial things and, perhaps, just thinks she is in love.

ELEONORE. So you accuse me of being untender?

FELIX. Of course.

ELEONORE. So you are sensitive as well.

FELIX. I have never doubted it.

ELEONORE. But I have.

FELIX. So now you know better.

ELEONORE. When one loves, it is easy for one to be annoying.

FELIX. The friend of the one you love does not let himself stand before you utterly unimportant.

ELEONORE. You have hurt me.

FELIX. Why did you force me to?

ELEONORE. Why do we always have to be so careful when we make use of someone a little?

FELIX. He who fails to stand up for himself when being put down is a fool.

ELEONORE. So I should be the one apologizing then.

FELIX. I am but a little ashamed, and now you may speak of him as much as you want. I will be rapt attention incarnate.

ELEONORE. I would no longer do so uninhibited.

FELIX. You know, on an island I would without hesitation give myself unconditionally to a woman. But we are among people whom we wish to always face again with ease and with the proper measure of self-respect.

ELEONORE. You are right, but what a shame it is this way.

FELIX. You do want to be seen as a respectable woman?

FRAU ELEONORE *shrugs her shoulders and remains silent for a while. She then assumes a cool and, from a formidable sense of superiority, petty air.*

[24]

For FELIX *a time lasting years came of dressing poorly. He faced many hardships.*

The day came when an offspring of cultured parents, in whom a girl believed too superficially, stabbed this girl to death. He stole the money she had on her to purchase proper clothing. Felix allowed girls to criticize the shortcomings of his appearance without giving it much thought. The girl above would have indulged the above young person as long as he could wear nice clothes. Perhaps her demise grew from such indulgence. For it is believed she made the indigent feel only silly, cheap, petty, superficial 'shock' when he no longer appeared 'noble' enough in her eyes. He became furious and took his revenge. Young ladies, take care that your boyfriends not only love you but respect you as well and make sure that you not just satisfy each other and wish and then no longer wish, then all over again, etc., but that you support each other when one or the other perhaps really needs it. By the way, I am convinced, and I often am, that a horrifically beautiful power forced him to kill. We are tools for making good or evil examples whose point of view we can, of course, argue about. Each one of us has experienced moments in which we turned into the prey of our own wallowing misanthropy. In such moments something like a marionette, something mechanical, claims us. Arms and legs and resolutions move according to dreadfully mathematical laws. It is possible that the girl knew the danger she was in, that she acted coquettishly with her fears and that, in the end, it was also her dalliance that incited him to commit his perfidious act. For a while Felix dressed in clothes that made a freak. The occasional impossibility of entering a cafe and being followed by glances of approval should not put us in too much of a bad mood. No, my friends, it cannot go that far. Felix, for example, wore the same hat for four years. Luckily, he wore it only in the countryside. But still, this hat and its long years of perseverance contributed rather much to the misinterpretation of fellow citizens. Then again, ladies would seek to engage him in conversation, those who recognize all such conveniences and learn to appreciate such situations. Felix was always busy. Our busyness should be that strong, capable of carrying us over many misfortunes. We should always commit to something. Otherwise it would be a great sin to direct the eyes of our cherished, fellow human beings, by means of anything so threadbare as to shock, were we to be left with no choice to think that we must not put it all on our suit without some reservations. Are these even serious observations? A few doubt it perhaps, which would not be a shame at all. That youngster who comes from a good home knew that he was damaging himself. Yes, gentlemen, if we are incapable of enduring and gradually making such damage right, could we not then be reproached for being lacking talent? He just stood there in the middle of the sun and his inferior clothes seemed more and more unwearable. This minor defect drove him to madness. He became nervous, which means evil. We can surely become horrible when our situation looks horrible. If we are horrified of ourselves, others will be horrified of us. I hope each one of you has actually experienced this. Please remember it. To kill such a quiet, delicate, I mean, such a breath of ability, how? Is it not in all of us? I mean, a very tenuous remnant of a gift dating back hundreds of years?? I ask myself. And ask you too. Neither of us knows whether it isn't something worse. You don't need to know what I mean by it. As long as you form your own opinion. Total, incomprehensible depravity does not exist. We can understand any aberration. Why must we so often turn little mistakes into such a hue and cry? That is because we are content with the discontent in others. O we evergreens—

Afterword

NO STANDING ROOM

Robert Walser's Theatre of Poetry and Fairy Tale

Be an outsider. Be a hero. Be Robert Walser.
Thomas Hirschhorn

The Serpent

In twentieth-century European literature, Robert Walser is a great loner. Born in the Swiss city of Biel in 1878, he began to apprentice at a banking house at the age of fourteen since his family could not afford to continue his education. After completing this apprenticeship, he undertook various odd jobs for banks and insurance companies and also started to write. His first works appeared in newspapers and magazines in 1898 and his first book was published in 1904. Over time, he began to make a living as a freelance writer, first in Zurich and Munich. He moved to Berlin in 1905, then returned to Biel in 1913, where he lived and worked until 1921 when he ended up in Bern.

Despite good reviews from critics and colleagues, including Franz Kafka, Robert Musil, Hermann Hesse and Walter Benjamin, he was not widely read. By the middle of the 1920s, he had even ceased to publish. Due to longstanding and continuing personal problems—he was 'desperate', 'totally written empty' and 'burnt out like an oven'[1]—he committed himself to Bern's Municipal Psychiatric Clinic in 1929. Then, in 1933, he was committed against his will to another sanatorium in the quiet resort town of Herisau in eastern Switzerland, where he gave up writing entirely and lived—in seclusion—for the next twenty-three years until he was found on Christmas Day, 1956, dead in the snow of an apparent heart attack while out on a walk.

A telling account of the last two decades of Walser's life may be found in Carl Seelig's memoir *Wanderungen mit Robert Walser* (1957), published just months after Walser's death. Along with its photo-graphs of Walser, which Seelig—his guardian and executor—took during their joint excursions, it provides the world with the public image of the writer. The surviving conversations, however, make for a sad record. Everything Walser loved and cherished had been smashed to pieces by National Socialism, thus casting a further pall over his being a writer to whom success had been denied. Wistfully perceptive, Walser relives his career. Failure was 'a furious, pernicious serpent', as it sought 'to strangle what was genuine and original in artists'.[2]

That Walser's international reputation would be established was not predictable either during his lifetime or after his death. And for a long time to come, it would be unthinkable that influential writers and intellectuals such as Susan Sontag, J. M. Coetzee, W. G. Sebald, Enrique Vila-Matas, Elfriede Jelinek, Giorgio Agamben, Tacita

1 Carl Seelig, *Wanderungen mit Robert Walser* (Frankfurt: Suhrkamp, 1977), p. 26. Also available as Carl Seelig, *Walks with Walser* (Ann Posten trans.) (New York: New Directions, 2017).

2 Seelig, *Wanderungen mit Robert Walser*, p. 66.

Dean, Rosemarie Trockel, Thomas Hirschhorn and Thomas Schütte would, one day, be discussing his books in leading publications around the world. Both his literary originality and his distance from established culture, and the *business* of culture (which ultimately led to his silence), have resulted in him now being regarded as the great outsider among the moderns. And a nonconformist and peripheral figure from another time has been transformed into a 'person of interest', into a 'writer's writer', into the embodiment of that modern artist who pays a high price for one's autonomy.

Although his language and themes are easily accessible, Walser's work is not so easily understood; it is work that refuses to fall into line, filled as it is with irony and caprice, digressions of narrative, provocative commonplaces and vexing turns of phrase that toy with a 'disciplined' reader's expectations. Often, one cannot tell what a text is about nor where it is going. Walser knows, better than most, how to work with the dynamics of language, as though the telling of a story were enough on its own, as though it could essentially stand without a subject. His tone remains unique in the way a musician can be unique. Walser, according to photographer and film-maker Robert Frank, reminds us of no other.

A Stubborn Dream

In 1914, Walser's 'Letter from a Poet to a Gentleman' was published in the magazine *Die Zukunft* (The Future),[3] in which a young poet responded to an 'honoured Sir' about why he would rather not have any contact with him, despite his being a willing patron, a benefactor.

3 Robert Walser, 'Brief eines Dichters an einen Herrn' [Letter from a Poet to a Gentleman] in *Kleine Dichtungen* [Prose Sketches] in *Sämtliche Werke* [Collected Works] (Jochen Greven ed.) (Frankfurt: Suhrkamp, 1985), VOL. 4, pp. 4–10.

As an 'eccentric' and a 'man on the street', the poet would prefer to live in his 'den of thieves'. With an outright refusal that may seem impertinent, the poet defends his freedom—only if he is independent and self-determined is he himself, and only if he is himself can he exist for others. That his conduct will offend the elegant gentleman, the poet takes in his stride, for 'One is always rude when one tells the truth.'

The poet ends his letter with a confession:

> I love the stars, and the moon is my secret friend. Above me is the sky. So long as I live, I will never forget to look up at them. I stand on the earth: this is my standpoint. These hours banter with me and I banter with them. I cannot think of a more delightful entertainment. Day and night are my companions. I love intimate walks with the evening and the morning. And with that, a poor young poet sends his greetings.

One should not confuse this 'poor young poet'—who so openly describes his point of view—with the author who hides behind him. At the time, Walser was no longer young—he was thirty-six and had returned to Biel from Berlin where he had published extensively and was on the verge of success. The 'poor young poet' is not Walser himself but an alter ego. Since Walser knew only too well what it was to be moulded by socioeconomic circumstances, self-sufficiency—autonomy—was not a given for him but a stubborn dream, a utopia.

The departure from the cultural metropolis of Berlin and the subsequent return to Biel in 1913 was not entirely a step backward. The tranquillity of his hometown allowed Walser to recover from the efforts and demands of competing in the world—and business—of culture, and immerse himself in what he saw as a writer's life, a way of life that increasingly informed his subject matter. He made writing, language and storytelling part of the theme, the materiality of pen and paper as well as the economic and everyday circumstances of a person who was both a private and a public figure. For the figure of the marginalized poet discloses its effect, subsequently, not only for readers but also vis-à-vis Walser himself, who serves as his own foil, field of possibility and surface on which to project. This surface is adapted to hold and maintain his literary identity—and becomes a part of it.

Meanwhile, in politics, dominated by nationalist and hegemonic imperatives, other forces began to affect the relativation and individualization of entrenched world views. And Walser created a poetic time–space based on perception and imagination, thus putting modern physics in parallel with the common notions of space and time in the human mind. Walser's profligate poet and Einstein's hypothetical observer both achieve insights that run diametrically opposed to prevailing ideas.

Walking Is Essential

The romantic element that grounds Walser's commitment in the real world is not present by chance. His obeisance to nature points towards tradition, which is sacred to him. For all the modernity attributed to him today, he himself never wanted to be modern. This was true for his manner of dress as it was for his books which he preferred to see printed in Gothic *Fraktur*. He knew where he came from, in part because he was a great reader—his poetic wilfulness is from the daydreams of Jean-Jacques Rousseau and Romanticism's

Taugenichts, from Eichendorff's *The Memoirs of a Good-for-Nothing* as well as from Georg Büchner's Lenz and Charles Baudelaire's Flaneur.

And Walser is just as familiar with the open countryside as he is with the library of world literature and the jungle of the big city. At home, however, he is in none of these worlds but on the road—his novel *Der Spaziergang* (The Walk), written in Biel in 1917, is a paean to the experience of walking. (The German title imparts more than the English, for at once it infers all forms of walking—for pleasure, health, observation and so on.)

By walking, this most basic form of mobility, Walser subtly sets in motion a seemingly fixed world. It suits him to playfully distort an established ritual in order to be persuasive as an artist:

> Walking is essential to me so that I may invigorate myself and maintain my connection with the living world, without whose feeling I could write no more than half a letter nor compose the least poem in verse or prose. Without walking I would be dead and my calling, which I love dearly, would be destroyed. [. . .] On a beautiful and circuitous walk a thousand useful thoughts come to mind. Locked inside the house, I would miserably fall apart and wither away. For me, walking is not only healthy and beautiful but also conducive and beneficial.[4]

Remaining in motion is Walser's nature. Living in Bern and changing his residence every few months, he wrote in 1926:

> Several of my fellow human beings go on long journeys via rail and ship and are naturally able to make impressive acquaintances and arrive upon all these expedient world

4 Walser, *Der Spaziergang* [The Walk] in *Sämtliche Werke*, VOL. 5, p. 50.

> views. I content myself with being a nomad in our city limits, a migratory species who is quite hale it seems, for I appear, from what I can tell, to be relatively healthy, i.e. it seems that I'm thriving.[5]

To be neither settled nor stationary describes not only Walser as an individual but also Walser as an artist: 'Why do you artists find no real rest anywhere and with any domestic setting?' he asked in 1916. 'Are you perhaps these conspicuous landmarks of restlessness, rich in unrest, poor, tossed back and forth by some longing for this other, never satisfied, forever insatiable, humankind as utterly unhappy?'[6] So it is not surprising that in Walser's eyes perception does not stand still. 'Things quintessential are not stationary,' we read in a 1927 essay, 'they wander instead.'[7]

The Presence of Reality

The quality of Walser's work is primarily based in his clever and deftly elaborate use of language. Vincent van Gogh is not famous because he painted sunflowers but because of the brilliant style with which he painted them. Walser's aura, too, is not found in the seemingly trivial things he wrote about but in his literary performance, the writing *itself*. That is what sets him apart. What he describes and recounts appears in a 'distant–nearness', is immediately present and simultaneously unreal, is transported. For him, literary fiction is an

5 Walser, 'Wohnungswechsel' [Change of Address] in *Wenn Schwache sich für stark halten: Prosa aus der Berner Zeit 1921–1925* [When a Weakling Regards Himself as Strong: Prose from the Bern Period, 1921–1925] in *Sämtliche Werke*, VOL. 17, p. 80.

6 Walser, *Der Spaziergang*, p. 35.

7 Walser, 'Spezialplatte' [Presentation Platter] in *Es war einmal: Prosa aus der Berner Zeit 1927–1928* [Once Upon a Time: Prose from the Bern Period, 1927–1928] in *Sämtliche Werke*, VOL. 19, p. 173.

integral part of reality, as are thoughts and dreams. His writing focuses not only on people and nature but also on their representation and the narrative itself. His earliest prose piece from 1899, 'Der Greifensee' (titled after a lake near Zurich) underscores the inherent dynamics of his storytelling—in it, 'springing over trails, meadows, forest, streams and fields' is personified and even given to speech: 'I come to no words, even though I already make for too many words. I don't know what I should say, for everything is so beautiful [. . .]'. Whereupon the narrator comes to the conclusion that the 'description speaks of such a way, in truth: an enthusiastic, enraptured description. And yet what should I say? I must speak like it [. . .]'.[8]

It was in the artificial expression of the theatre that Walser intensely experienced the presence of reality. His 1907 essay, 'Das Theater, ein Traum' [The Theatre, a Dream], commingled the interior of the theatre with the bedroom, for the immediacy of the theatre is the same as the dream:

> Are they not the dreams of poetry, and is the open stage something other than its enormous opening, like a mouth talking in its sleep? While these demanding times drive us through the streets and locales of our affairs and expediencies, we find ourselves then in these narrow rows of seats as though in narrow beds watching and listening. The curtain, the lip of that mouth, rises and roars, hisses, flickers and laughs for us in a way that estranges and is likewise confidential. It arouses us with an arousal we could control and may not. It makes us double up in laughter or shake from weeping inside ourselves. The images blaze and burn before

8 Walser, 'Der Greifensee' [Griffin Lake] in *Geschichten* [Stories] in *Sämtliche Werke*, VOL. 2, p. 33, p. 34.

> our eyes. Before us the characters of the play move with a supernatural size like shapes never before seen. The bedroom is dark. Only the open dream glows in its stark light, blinding, speaking, as it forces one, with open mouth, to sit for it.[9]

For Walser, literature is not a dead letter but a living discourse. Reality does not exist detached from his perception and representation. Literature is a performative moment—it is an event that creates reality and expands and changes through fresh, new perspectives.

Theatre without a Stage

In his youth, Walser was inspired by Friedrich Schiller and dreamt of becoming an actor and playwright. This was true also of his brother Karl, a stage designer whose success in Berlin certainly attracted Robert, the younger by a year. Despite the family connection to the theatre and an admiration for the theatre which he expressed in his essays, Walser did not write for the stage. Even the dramolettes, published here in a complete edition for the first time in English, were not intended to be performed in any kind of theatrical setting. They were, rather, intended to be read, to be closet dramas as Walser explained to his publishers Ernst Rowohlt and Kurt Wolff in 1912:

> They are entirely poetry and definitely only for the aesthetic enjoyment of adults. They are anchored in style and beauty, and the main thing is the pleasure of the book. If

9 Walser, 'Das Theater, ein Traum' [The Theatre, a Dream] in *Bedenkliche Geschichten: Prosa aus der Berliner Zeit 1906–1913* [Critical Writings: Prose from the Berlin Period, 1906–1913] in *Sämtliche Werke*, VOL. 15, p. 8ff.

> they could be performed with music is utterly doubtful and for the present totally irrelevant. They are tempered for speech and language, for cadence and rhythmic pleasure. [10]

Indeed, the interest in Walser's dramolettes came decades later, in the 1970s, when they were first staged by young, experimental theatre troupes and theatres in Germany, France and Switzerland. A milestone in the history of their reception is Heinz Holliger's opera *Schneewittchen*, based on Walser's adaptation of 'Snow White', which the Zurich Opera premiered in 1998 and the Basel Theatre more recently staged in 2014.

Walser published two of his earliest dramolettes in 1901 in *Die Insel* (Island), a German avant-garde magazine, at a time when the short dramatic form was popular and cultivated by authors such as Oscar Wilde, Selma Lagerlöf and Hugo von Hofmannsthal. Apparently, Walser still had a high regard for his early works, for *Schneewittchen* and *Aschenbrödel* ('Cinderella') appeared with *Die Knaben* ('The Boys') and *Dichter* ('Poets')—plays written no later than 1900—under the title *Komödie* (Comedies) in book form in 1919. Although this volume received practically no critical response, Walser wrote more dramolettes, and *Der Taugenichts* ('The Good-for-Nothing'), *Das Liebespaar* (The Lovers), *Dornröschen* ('Thorn Rose, or The Sleeping Beauty') and *Das Christkind* ('The Christ Child') were all composed and published in literary journals between 1920 and 1922. His dramatic production continued in 1924 and 1925, resulting in *Felix Szenen* ('The "Felix" Scenes'), written in pencil and in the tiny and seemingly encrypted micrographic script that Walser used to put his final works to paper from 1924 onwards.

10 Walser to Ernst Rowohlt in *Briefe* [Letters] (Jörg Schäfer and Robert Mächler eds) (Frankfurt: Suhrkamp, 1979).

(Among these are nearly forty additional dramatic scenes, which lie outside the scope of this volume.)

Another exceptional—and early work—is *Der Teich* ('The Pond'). It is truly an outlier for it is the only instance of Walser writing a literary work in his native Swiss dialect. This brief family drama is autobiographical and was given as a gift to Walser's younger sister Fanny in 1902. Not intended for publication, it was found among Walser's papers and published in 1972 along with 'The "Felix" Scenes' and the novel *Der Räuber* ('The Robber').

The dramolettes published during his lifetime made virtually no impression on readers and critics. One exception is, however, Walter Benjamin's 1929 essay 'Robert Walser'.[11] According to Benjamin, Walser showed how fairy tales could still 'live'; looking back over the first quarter of the twentieth century, Benjamin considered the dramolette 'Snow White' to be 'one of the profoundest works of new writing' and that it 'alone would suffice to make people understand why this apparently most playful of all poets had been a favourite author of merciless Kafka'.

In reality, the dramolettes occupy a special place in Walser's opus. They are a kind of magical literary theatre, a 'total poetry'.[12] Their characters, who reflect their roles and are aware of their literary status, embody the modern individual and so understand the conditions of their own existence. To them, the text is their world and life, and the language from which they exist is their nature. And Walser represents this self-awareness as an eccentric state of lyrical

11 Walter Benjamin, 'Robert Walser' in *Illuminationen: Ausgewählte Schriften* [*Illuminations: Selected Writings*] (Siegfried Unseld ed.) (Frankfurt: Suhrkamp, 1961), VOL. 1, pp. 349–52.

12 Or *ganz Poesie*, Walser to Rowohlt in *Briefe*, p. 59.

exaltation. When the characters discuss their existence—as though in a state of poetic ecstasy–madness—it is as if they were standing beside themselves. Everything has already happened. Time has stopped for a moment. Life has been stretched out for examination. Life has become a dream reality that is fantastic, disillusioning, demonic, enchanting, enlightening and uplifting all at the same time.

In addition to the subject matter and its meta-theatrical dimension, there is Walser's inimitable voice that gives the dramolettes their special charm. Despite their elegant simplicity, they are full of surprising and ironic twists and turns of phrase. In 'Cinderella', the Prince finds a suitable image to express this:

> The language must be a weasel
> falling headlong when it wishes [. . .].

In the wake of our postmodern flood of images and that concomitant virtualization that accompanies them, the unreality of images is seen with a critical eye. De-realization implies a threatening form of alienation as well as innovation and 'coolness'. In 'Thorn Rose, or the Sleeping Beauty', fiction would almost seem to be that seductive and romantic power that allows one to transform reality:

> Isn't reality a dream too?
> Aren't we all, even when awake,
> going about something like dreamers,
> sleepwalkers in the light of day,
> who but play with what comes to mind
> and act as if awake?
> Well, we are, but what is being awake?

While they have this playful effect, the dramolettes—especially the fairy-tale kind—are canny and economic didactic set pieces as well. Their characters find themselves twisting and turning in a purgatory of verse until they confess, which is their mission. They are messengers of a poetic existence that evinces a human desire for delimitation and localization, that is, for wanting no place and wanting a place too. As an enlightened poet, Walser knew where the power of poetry lay. The Fairy Tale herself explains it in 'Cinderella':

> I came here to leave you in awe.
> People do not believe in me,
> but so what when just my being near
> makes them think a little again.

Moving Beauty

As Walser's work stands crosswise to the mainstream, its beauty is hardly dead. At a time when the aesthetics of the ugly and the uncomfortably strange are in demand, Walser's work is unapologetically about 'pretty' things—landscapes, boys, girls, forests, Mozart, lakes, villages, the moon and the stars. His changes in perspective and tone prevent the beautiful from appearing flat or naive. And his subtle irony, which does not shy away from humour, affects and moves the reader without being sentimental—or, in the plays, dramaturgical and histrionic—in the classical sense.

Following its master narrative, *Der Spaziergang* at the end of 1917, *Poetenleben* (Lives of Poets) begins with its own poetological contemplation of walking as an art. While walking, the beautiful appears bound to one's self and thus sets the world in motion. The poet's perception connects 'everything that is strange and beautiful' to an animated stream of impressions 'as I progressed this way, as the whole round world effortlessly moves along with me, it happened. Everything seemed to wander with the wanderer: meadows, fields, forests, clearings, mountains, even the road itself.'[13]

Not only is nature beautiful but playing children too, musicians, labourers and any kind of everyday object worth looking at. *Poetenleben* features long discourses on a stove and a button, celebrating their humble and utilitarian existence as though they were the works of old masters. Things to write about exist everywhere and nowhere for the poet:

> Thoughtfully, I stood in the room. Suddenly I saw something world-weary hanging onto something weary of life.
>
> It was just about falling from its hole, which no longer properly held, a tired, ancient nail, on which hung an umbrella just about as old and battered.
>
> To see how something old and woebegone clutched onto something old and woebegone, to see and observe how something decrepit hung on to something else decrepit, as though they were two beggars embracing in some cold, hopeless wasteland so as to perish pressed closely together, prepared to die at any moment.
>
> To see how something weak in its weakness still supported something else weak before it completely slipped away in its powerlessness, and how this pathetic thing in its lamentably pathetic state offered for so long to still hold up this other pathetic thing at least a little as though it would have exhausted itself in the end, moved and shook me deeply, and I would not want to miss recording it here.[14]

13 Walser, *Poetenleben* [Lives of Poets] in *Sämtliche Werke*, VOL. 6, p. 7.

14 Walser, *Poetenleben,* p. 105ff.

Beauty lies not in significant and important things but, rather, in the poet who turns to something marginal in order to make it something larger and significant through the power of words, like a magician. It is not the particular and the sublime that is moving but life itself whose real significance becomes experiential through art.

Republic of Poets

Although social and moral issues of his time concerned him, Walser avoided matters of everyday life and party politics. Nevertheless, his interest in the material circumstances of the writing life and his unconventional views of the establishment do give his writing a political dimension. He came from a modest background and milieu, and wrote about little people, ordinary things and hierarchical relationships. He also ironized the established culture and subverted the conventions of the bourgeois world with his radically independent perception.

'The more horror filled this world (like now), the more abstract the art,' wrote Paul Klee in his diary in 1915 as the First World War raged across Europe. For this reason, the 'cool romanticism' of modern art, its 'style without pathos', had an enormous effect on Klee—and in his own work, Walser also relativized and transcended the romantic ideal to a world that was already changing before the war. Walser relativized and transcended the romantic ideal. But he did so without being abstract. Instead, he made the concrete circumstances of his work his theme, such that it resembles a vast tableau of—and for—writing: the paper and pen, the things to read and the inspiration, the time and the room, the money and pleasure, the writing in itself and the novel in itself, the writing for the feuilletons, the reader and the narrator—everything is made into a theme and leads towards an enormous narrative that for Walser was 'a multifariously dissected or sliced-up self-book'.[15] Sociologist Max Weber, writing in 1917, described an 'iron cage', this ever-advancing mechanization and rationalization as this 'disenchantment-and-demystification of the world', a development that Walser worked against insofar as he made his everyday reality into poetry.

'I stand on this earth: this is my standpoint.' Being on his own, exposed to life with this intent, to respond to a reality becoming ever more matter of fact with poetry—this for Walser was what a writer should do. For once expressing himself politically, albeit ironically, he writes: 'Our form of government is a republic. We are allowed to do whatever we want.'[16] Walser is no political author. He does, however, make literature political in that he cultivates the stubbornness of the individual and the power of the imagination. The world is the result of different ideas and expectations, that which one makes of it—always new, always different.

Reto Sorg
Robert Walser–Zentrum, Bern

15 Walser, 'Eine Art Erzählung' [A Kind of Tale] in *Für die Katz: Prosa aus der Berner Zeit 1918–1933* [For the Cat: Prose from the Bern Period, 1918–1933] in *Sämtliche Werke*, VOL. 20, p. 322.

16 Walser, 'Das Vaterland' [The Fatherland] in *Fritz Kochers Aufsätze* [Fritz Kocher's Essays] in *Sämtliche Werke*, VOL. 1, p. 30.